Joseph Petrus Wergin

Win at Cribbage

Oldcastle Books

1993

Oldcastle Books

18 Coleswood Rd

Harpenden,Herts,AL5 1EQ

A CIP catalogue record for this book is available from the British Library.

[U.S. bibliographic information - Includes index. 1. Cribbage I. Title.
GV 1295.C9W47 795.4 79-17045]

I S B N 0 - 948353 - 97 - X   Win at Cribbage [2nd edition]

9 8 7 6 5 4 3 2 1

Printed and bound by Guernsey Press

Typeset by Screentext.

Distributed in the U.S.A. by Wergin Distributors, P.O.Box 5584. Madison,
WI 53705.

Dedicated io the Grass Root players who responded to the author's call to form clubs in local communities, thus providing a training ground for future great players. This enthusiastic reaction is making Cribbage the leading card game in America.

The author acknowledges the valuable assistance rendered by the following individuals in the preparation of the Revised Edition.

* ALLAN LICHTY
  for his charts and records of thousands of games

* KEN CAMBELL, LARRY and VIRGINIA WHITE
  for technical advice and editorial assistance

* DAVID PARLETT[1]
  for providing the Introduction

* THE GAMBLERS BOOK CLUB,
  Publisher of Key to Cribbage, for permission to use copyrighted material

* KARL W. GRUBE,
  President, The International Gamester Ltd, for his remarks about the author.

* F. WILLIAM A. OTTERSTEIN, B.S., M.Ed., ME-PD., *and fellow Skat and Cribbage player, for his diligent attention to detail in proofreading WIN AT CRIBBAGE.*

[1] *England's Authority on card games*

ABOUT THE AUTHOR

Educator, Author, Tournament Director, Promoter, Friend of Youth are terms which describe JOSEPH PETRUS WERGIN, President Emeritus of the American Cribbage Congress as well as Commissioner for Cribbage under the auspices of *"World Mind Sports Olympiad"* who holds B.S. and M.S. Degrees in Education from the University of Wisconsin at Madison.

The year was 1979. The place Raleigh, North Carolina, USA. The game was tournament CRIBBAGE. Joe Wergin spoke in favor of a National Cribbage Organization which would standardize the rules of tournament Cribbage, provide a grass-roots approach to play, and promote the greatest two-handed game ever invented. JOSEPH PETRUS WERGIN'S ideas and energy crystallized the concept of a cribbage congress. This group now enjoys a reputation as the fastest growing playing card organization in North America.

"The Fox", as Joe Wergin is known to card players around the world, has designed and implemented cribbage tournament innovations which are now commonplace to seasoned North American cribbage players.

* Implemented Round Robin Play followed by Elimination Brackets.

* Established uniform examinations for qualifying Judges

* Designed the Long Board for Cribbage Tournaments

* Originated the idea of local Grass Roots Cribbage Clubs

* Authored the book, CRIBBAGE FOR KIDS

*   Designed a Cribbage educational board game

*   Conducted classes in Cribbage at Intermediary, Secondary, and University Schools.

Perhaps the best accolade to Joseph Petrus Wergin appears in a quote found in the illustrated children's work, CRIB-BAGE FOR KIDS.

If you play cribbage, by all means teach your children to play. It is not only a game of numbers but it also trains the young learner to reason out situations and to make logical decisions....The beauty of the game is that grade school children can play well enough to win over grandparents.

A Tribute to a Visionary

Karl W. Grube, Ph.D., President/CEO
The International Gamester, Ltd.
Ann Arbor, MI USA

ABOUT THE GAME

What needs to be said about a card game invented by a seventeenth-century British poet and played by 2 or 3 million Americans each night?

Sir John Suckling--best known for his "Song" which begins "Why so pale and wan, fond lover?"--built upon the elements of an older game, Noddy, and created "Cribbage" sometime between 1632 and 1639. Today, Cribbage is immensely popular on both sides of the Atlantic. Combining the intellectual challenge of a game of strategy with the excitement and surprise of a game of chance, Cribbage is known by its millions of enthusiasts as the greatest two-handed game in the world of cards.

In the past ten years, the knowledge of scientific play has risen to new heights. Detailed play of thousands and thousands of games has been charted. Regional tournaments, which are now commonplace, have brought master players together for head-to-head competition. Intricate plays, maneuvres, and traps that are in a top-rated player's repertoire are amazing and unbelievable.

In this book, an internationally known expert shares his winning secrets with the reader. *Win at Cribbage* has been designed as a complete, step-by-step course. It should prove equally valuable to the beginner and to the experienced player who seeks mastery of the game. Read it, study it-- and win!

INTRODUCTION

by

David Parlett

The great thing about a deck of cards is its tremendous versatility. Once upon a time there were five card players marooned on a desert island. They were getting along fine with their Poker sessions, but a poisonous snake bit the four-flusher and then there were just enough left for Contract Bridge. One night a coconut landed square on dummy's skull and then there were three. So they stripped out all ranks lower than seven and got cracking on Skat. Soon after, the timidest member of the trio got away with a grand solo against four and promptly died of heart failure. Several months later, when we rescued the Solitaire player, the first thing he said was, "It's a good thing we didn't throw those low-spotters away." "What do you mean?" we asked him. "Hell, have you ever tried playing Cribbage without the fives?"

Well, if you've never played this great two-hander the unorthodox way then I suggest you turn to the story about fooling the old chemistry teacher. And if you've never played it at all--now's the time to get started.

Next to Shakespeare, Cribbage has always struck me as perhaps England's greatest contribution to western civilization, which makes me particularly pleased to have been invited to introduce this latest study of the skills (and fun) involved.

Cribbage is essentially a battle of wits with figures, and I can think of no one more qualified than Joe Wergin to take the back off and show you how it ticks. I daresay more people play Cribbage than Skat (especially in England, where the latter is virtually unknown), but I can tell you that Wergin on Skat and Sheepshead has been my favorite and most profitable reading for as long as I can remember. Not for nothing is he known as the Old Fox at the card table. Few people earn a twin reputation as champion player and eminently readable writer. But Joe Wergin is one of them, and once you get dipping into Win at Cribbage you'll see I'm not exaggerating. Especially when you sit down at your next session.

Good cribbing!

David Parlett of Surrey England, is The World's Leading Authority on the History of Card Games.

CONTENTS

CHAPTER I

FUNDAMENTALS

HOW TO LEARN CRIBBAGE

When you are ready to learn Cribbage, I suggest you purchase a piece of furniture, a Cribbage board. It is used to keep the running score.

Before securing a teacher for yourself, I recommend that you prepare by reading the following pages. Cribbage, a game of English origin, may be placed in the category of games of combinations, which includes Poker, Old Maid, and the various forms of Rummy. You undoubtedly know how to shuffle the cards and how to play several other card games, but a knowledge of those games will be of little help because Cribbage is unusual.

Standard Deck

Before you start, take a regular fifty-two-card deck and lay cards face up on the table for study, because most people are eye-minded. Actually see the card combinations instead of trying to visualize them in your mind.

Cribbage has some special terms which you must become familiar with.

Deal Out Hands

After you have read the first two parts, play some practice games by yourself. Deal six cards to each of two hands, one card at a time. Figure out the point combinations and discard two cards into the dealer's crib.

Peg the Points

Peg on the Cribbage board the points each hand scores for you and an imaginary opponent. Then count the points of the crib cards and peg the crib points on the dealer's part of the board. Repeat this over and over until you can count the points of hands quickly. (On the first deal, you may omit the play of the hand, which occurs after the starter card is determined by the cutting of the pack. See Chapter II.)

The Cribbage Board

The scoring board for Cribbage was patterned after the Noddy board (Noddy is thought to be the forerunner of Cribbage).

A Cribbage board has two rows of 30 holes plus a game hole for each player, making a total of 61 holes for each player. Each line of 30 holes is divided into six groups of 5 holes for easier scoring. The board was designed for the original five-card game in which 61 points won, and the first player to arrive at the game hole with his scoring peg was the winner.

In the modern six-card game, the players must make two trips around the board with their pegs, plus the game hole, scoring 121 points to win.

The Long Board

For centuries man has been trying to make a better mouse-trap, and many contraptions have been invented. But we still have mice.

Two trips around the traditional board confuses many players when 21 qualifying games are played. They lose their sense of direction as to which street they are on. This writer knew that there had to be a better board for tournament play.

The long board was designed to eliminate pegging errors and simplify the pegging process. It was first used in the Madison Masters Classic and it became popular immediately. The progress of a game is easy to follow and the board is very useful in charting and studying position play.

Practically, all club and tournament play is recorded on a long board.

If the original game consisted of six cards instead of five, Sir John Suckling would have designed this board in the beginning.

Use Your Spare Time

Spend your daily free time on this learning project, dealing out the cards and analyzing them. Then advance to playing out the hands and pegging as you go along.

Next, find an experienced player or teacher so that you can play your first game.

Refer Back to Book

Play as much Cribbage as possible and be sure to read and reread the material in this book. Also, discuss hands and methods of play selection with veteran players.

Continue dealing out hands to yourself and memorize combinations so that you can quickly announce the points your hand scores. This will make you a welcome opponent.

Play, play, play, and be sure to refer back to the book. To my German friends I as Der Fuchs (The Fox) say: "Arbeit macht dein Meister!" Or in English, practice makes perfect.

DEFINITIONS

Balk   *throwing two cards to dealer's crib which
                tend not to fit into combinations*

Board   *with peg holes is used to record the score*

Crib   *four cards laid to side for dealer*

Cut Jack   *jack turned up after pack is cut*

Dealing   *each of two players are dealt six cards,
                one at a time*

Deck   *the standard pack of 52 cards*

Deuce   *two-spot card*

Discard   *to lay aside two cards for crib*

Double run   *two three-card straights including a pair*

Fifteen-two   *count of cards totaling 15, two holes are
                scored on the board*

15/2   *symbol for fifteen-two*

Flush   *four or five cards of the same suit*

Game   *121 points in the six-card game; 61 points
                in the five-card game*

Game Hole   *hole no. 121 (no. 61 in five-card)*

Go   *the last card played under 31 or card that
                reaches 31 in pegging process*

His heels	*the cut jack; jack, when it is turned for starter card (two points to turner)*
His nobs	*the right jack; jack in hand, same suit as starter card (one point to holder)*
Lurch	*to defeat opponent by 31 or more points; to skunk*
Knave	*jack*
Pair	*two cards of same denomination, as two queens*
Pair royal	*three of a kind (triplets)*
Peg	*metal, wood, or plastic pieces used to mark the score*
Pegging	*the act of moving the pegs in scoring*
Pip	*any of the spots on playing cards*
Playing off	*laying cards down that prevent sequences*
Pone	*the non-dealer*
Right jack	*jack, in hand, same suit as starter card (same as "nobs")*
Sequence	*straight of at least three cards, as nine, ten, jack*
Showing	*exposing the hand and counting the values*
Skunk	*losing by 31 or more holes; lurch*

Spotter	*the number of spots or pips, (clubs, hearts, diamonds, spades) on a card*
Starter card	*card turned up after pack is cut*
Stink hole	*hole no. 120, the last hole before going out*
Straight	*a run or sequence of three or more cards as seven, eight, nine*
Street, First	*consists of the first 30 holes*
Street, Second	*31st to 60th hole*
Street, Third	*61st to 90th hole*
Street, Fourth	*91st to 120th hole*
Tenth cards	*kings, queens, jacks, and tens, each have a value of 10 points*
Trey	*three spotter*
Valley cards	*eights, sevens, and sixes*
Winning	*scoring 121 holes before opponent*

Object

To score points by forming combinations of cards and win the six-card game by totaling 121 points before an opponent can do so.

MECHANICS OF CRIBBAGE

Number of Players

The basic game for two players is the most popular; however, Cribbage is also played three- and four-handed - the latter being a partnership affair, two against two.

Cards Used

The standard deck of fifty-two cards is used. Each player receives six cards on the deal.

Distributing the Cards

The dealer is chosen by cutting the cards; the player with the lower card deals. (The ace is the lowest card of all.) If there is a tie, cut again.

Shuffling and Cutting

Nondealer may shuffle the cards, but the dealer has the right to make the last shuffle. The pack must be cut once by the nondealer, leaving at least four cards in each packet.

The Las Vegas shuffle or riffle is best for mixing the cards.

Rank of the Cards - Point Count

The four suits are of equal rank and the cards rank from king down to ace (represented by 1):

```
         K - Q - J - 10 - 9 - 8 - 7 - 6 - 5 - 4 - 3 - 2 - 1
points:  10  10  10  10   9   8   7   6   5   4   3   2   1
```

The Crib

Each participant discards two cards into the crib or box, reducing his hand to four cards. The crib is the property of the dealer; it may not be examined or disturbed until after the play.

Starter Card

After both players have discarded, the pone (nondealer) cuts the pack and the dealer turns over the top card of the lower packet onto the table. The top packet is replaced on the lower packet and the turned-over card is placed face up on top. It is the starter card.

His Heels

If the starter is a jack (called the knave in England), the dealer scores 2 points. He must take (peg) them before he plays a card, or he forfeits the 2 points. The starter is not used in the play (Chapter III).

Be sure to read this book before your opponent does. Your honour and money will be saved!

Webster's says: "Card game for two, three, or four players in which the object is to form various combinations that count for points; the score is kept on a small peg board."

The jack or knave was originally called noddy; now it can be called his heels, his nobs, or his nibs.

CHAPTER II

THE PLAY

An outstanding characteristic of Cribbage is its two-step procedure: first the play, then the showing. The only scoring before the play is his heels (just discussed).

The pone begins play by selecting a card from his or her hand, and playing it face up on the table on his side of the board, and announcing its count value.

Example: Pone, the non-dealer, lays a trey down and says "Three".

Then the dealer lays down a card, stating the total of the two cards.

The dealer plays an eight and says, "Eleven" (not "Eight").

Now the pone places a second card on his stack, stating the total of all three cards played.

Note that each player keeps his cards separate and does not assemble them in tricks. He sets his cards down so as not to cover each other, all the cards played in the series must be visible.

SCORING FOR GO

Hit 31 and Peg 2 Points.....

One object of the play is to reach a total of exactly 31 on one

of your laydowns and score 2 points. You may not run the
count over 31.

If a player cannot lay down a card that will not exceed the
31 count, he says, "Go," which means "Go ahead! I cannot
play."

If his adversary can play one or more cards that will not
exceed the 31 mark, he must play them announcing the new
total or totals as he plays. If he has no eligible card, he says,
"Go" (or "Pass"). Some players knock on the table to signify
their inability to make a legal play.

Peg Only 1 Point for Last Card Played

If no one reaches exactly 31, the person laying down the last
card possible under 31 pegs 1 point.

Example 1:

COUNT	A HOLDS	B HOLDS
26	K-6	4-2

It is A's turn to play. The king would bring the total to 26
+ 10 = 36, and the six to 26 + 6 = 32. As he may not play either
card, A says, "Go".

Player B plays the four, making the count 30, and then
passes because the deuce would surpass 31. He pegs 1 point
for playing the last card.

Example 2:

COUNT	A HOLDS	B HOLDS
24	6-1	9-8

A lays down the six saying, "30." As B does not have an ace

to play, he says, "Go," and A continues by laying down his ace, hitting 31. He pegs 2 points.

When the series is completed by the first Go, both players may turn the cards already played face down to avoid confusion during the next series.

A new count working from 0 toward the goal of 31 is begun by the player whose turn it is. In Example 2, player A having made the last play with an ace, B opens the second series with his eights or his nine.

Play is continued until both competitors have used up all four cards. This is most vividly demonstrated in the cinema version of Sir James M. Barrie's novel *The Little Minister* showing a Cribbage match between brother and sister.

Count of 15

Fifteen is a magic number for Cribbage players, By making the playing count 15 a player pegs 2 points immediately. It is an important tactic to prevent an opponent from hitting the 15 mark.

Example: You hold Q-J-3-2.

If you lead off with the queen or jack for a count of 10, your opponent may play a five, totaling 15 and pegging 2 points. The logical lead is to play the three; opponent will stay under 15 no matter what card he plays.

Opponent probably has at least one of the 16 ten-counting cards in the deck (kings, queens, jacks, and tens). If he brings the count up to 13, you can play your deuce for 15.

It is possible to peg 3 points by playing the last card of the two hands and hitting the magic count of 15 at the same time: 2 points for the 15, and 1 for the last card.

SCORING FOR MATCHES AND SEQUENCES

	POINTS
Pair	2
Triplet	6
Quadruplet	12
Sequence of three cards	3
Sequence of four cards	4
Sequence of five cards	5 (etc)

Pair

By immediately matching the card played by your opponent, you peg 2 points, which must be racked up at once. You must pair rank as well as count: two kings are a pair, but a king and a queen are not, although they are both tenth cards.

Triplet

Three of a kind played in sequence score 6 points for the player who lays down the third card. Our English cousins, as well as early Americans, call the triplet a pair royal. However, it all means one thing.....6 points for the fortunate competitor, and humilation for the opponent who played the second card, making only 2 points for a pair.

Example: Player A plays a six; B lays down a second six and pegs 2 point for a pair; A retaliates with a third six for 6 big points.

Four of a Kind (Double Pair Royal)

Continuing the example, if B has the fourth six, he comes roaring back to form a quadruplet and peg 12 points, for a very grand total of 2 + 12= 14 points, far outscoring A's six points.

Four of a kind is very rare and its high score of 12 obeys a law of frequency: the less often a hand occurs, the more it will scores.

Sequence

All Poker addicts appreciate the value of sequences (also called straights or runs) in their battle of wits. There are straights in Cribbage too, including three-card straights, four-card straights, and Pokerlike straights. You get 1 point credit for each card in the sequence.

A sequence can be played in a juggled order such as 4-2-3, which is a legal sequence.

Eleven Three-Card Runs

The basic three-card sequences are the following:

1-2-3	5-6-7	9-10-J
2-3-4	6-7-8	10-J-Q
3-4-5	7-8-9	J-Q-K
4-5-6	8-9-10	

Each basic sequence has six forms: for example, 4-5-6, 4-6-5, 5-4-6, 5-6-4, 6-4-5, and 6-5-4.

Kings and aces are never included in the same run; there is no such run as Q-K-A or K-A-2.

Six Four-Card Straights

The basic four-card straights, each of which can be juggled in 24 orders of play, are:

1-2-3-4	4-5-6-7
2-3-4-5	5-6-7-8
3-4-5-6	6-7-8-9

The 6-7-8-9 sequence makes a count of 30 in the pegging process. It is impossible to use 7-8-9-10 or higher four-card combinations in the play, since they add up to more than 31 points.

A Sequence with a Go

If a straight is formed, and the count of 31 is reached at the same time, the player receives 2 points for making 31 as well as the points for ending the run.

Example: This four-card run ends at 31.

card played	count	pegging
7	7	-
J	17	-
3	20	-
2	22	-
5	27	-
4	31	6

The player who reaches 31 gets 2 pegging points for Go and 4 more points for the run of four cards 3-2-5-4, or in its basic form, 2-3-4-5.

Go with a Seven-Card Sequence

Straights may include as many as seven cards. Suppose the first six cards are juggled: 7-5-2-4-3-6. There is no run until the fifth card, when the trey player scores 4 points for 5-2-4-3. When his opponent counters with the six-spotter, a six-card run is formed for 6 points. An ace after the six will make a seven-card run for 7 holes.

As shown below, a seven-card run can mean 7 points plus.

cards played	count	pegging	
3	3	-	
7	10	-	
5	15	2	(15/2)
2	17	-	
3	20	-	
4	24	4	(run of four)
1	25	5	(run of five)
6	31	9	(run of seven & Go of 31)

An eight-card straight is unplayable because the lowest such straight has a count of 36 (which is over 31).

(Note that the second trey played did not score 2 points for a pair, because it was not played immediately after the first trey.)

Simultaneous Pegging

When you play a card that brings the count on the table to 31, you may also get credit for other, simultaneous scoring plays.

Example 1: A pair is formed. If the count is 23 and play of a four makes 27, the play of a second four hits 31 and makes a pair, so the player scores 4 holes - 2 for the 31 and 2 for the pair.

Example 2: Three of a kind with a go.

	count	pegging
A lays down a jack	10	-
B pairs him with another jack	20	2
A counters with a third jack	30 & go	7

Neither player holds an ace, so 30 ends the series. A scores 1 point for the go and 6 points for the triplets, a total of 7 holes.

Note: Pairs, triplets, and sequences may end with the Go. Suppose the count stands at 13, A lays down a nine bringing the count to 22, and B makes 31 with his nine, scoring 4 points - 2 for the 31 and 2 for the pair.

The next series starts, and A has another nine-spotter and leads off with it. He cannot claim a score of 6 for triplets, even though three nines were played in succession. He gets no points for the nine.

Example 3: Pegging with quadruplets.

Someday it will happen to you - pegging 12 by lining up four sevens in a row. With 2 holes for the pair and 1 for a go, you can score 15 points in one series of play, which your opponent scores 6 for triplets.

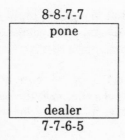

8-8-7-7

pone

dealer

7-7-6-5

Pone plays a seven, dealer pairs, scoring 2 holes, and pone retaliates with a third seven making the count 21 and scoring 6 holes for triplets.

Dealer counters with the fourth seven scoring 12 for four of a kind and takes another point for the go.

The dealer now has in effect five cards: the four he has just used in the play, plus the starter card. Likewise the nondealer (pone) has in effect five cards, including the same starter card.

The crib, the third hand which scores for the dealer, has in effect five cards: the same starter card, the two cards discarded before the play by the play by the dealer, and the two cards discarded before the play by the pone.

Note that (1) the crib took no part in the play; (2) the dealer and nondealer no longer play out cards against each other but simply score their own hands; first, the pone's hand; second, the dealer's own hand; and third, the dealer's second (crib) hand.

RULES EVERYONE SHOULD KNOW

Trust everyone but cut the cards!

THE FIRST DEALER

Cut the pack and low card deals with the ace being low. In multi-game matches, the loser deals first for the next game.

SHUFFLING

Riffle the pack two or three times and finish with an over and under.

CUTTING THE PACK

The pack MUST be cut taking off at least four cards and leaving at least four.

In the cut for the Starter Card, a person may not look at the bottom card. The penalty is two points.

After the cut, the two packets must be reunited before the cards are dealt out.

In cutting for the starter card if the cut card is face up, turn it over and reshuffle that portion of the pack and cut again for a starter.

DEALING

If a card is exposed in the dealing process redeal. However, if pone causes a card to be upturned, complete the deal.

Do not pick the cards up until dealer has completed the distribution, as a courtesy to the dealer.

PEGGING

When you take your hand off the peg, the pegging is completed.

If you peg short of the mark, the points are lost.

If you take up your front peg to record a score, the back peg immediately becomes the front peg.

If you peg in the wrong direction, too bad, the pegs stand as placed.

If both pegs fall out and you and your opponent cannot agree where they were, call a Judge.

If you peg too many points and your opponent calls you on it, your front peg is moved back to the correct spot and your opponent receives that amount of points as a penalty.

If you peg too many points and your peg is placed in the Game Hole thus claiming the game the following procedure takes place: note: a colon indicates a series is yet to follow!

1. Your peg is placed in the correct hole.
2. Your opponent receives the extra point or points taken.
3. You are then penalized 15 points backward from your front peg.

After completing the first series in pegging towards 31, the cards may not be turned over.

MUGGINS

If you are allowed to take points that an adversary over-looks, it is called "muggins," which is what you call out to announce your claim. The innovation is optional.

This variation is not a part of the game. Family and club groups do not use the option, as it is believed that missing points is penalty enough.

Also muggins slows down the counting process. It takes longer to play a game because contestants take so much time counting, recounting, checking, and rechecking every hand to avoid a double loss of points. Muggins gives the veteran an unwarranted advantage over an inexperienced player.

Another objection to muggins is that it is frustrating and exasperating for one who is trying to enjoy a recreational activity, to be doubly penalized for a simple error.

Author's favourite saying: "I play Cribbage the old-fashioned way. I EARN my points."

CHAPTER III

THE SHOWING

HOW TO COUNT FOR THE SHOWING

The order of scoring is important and the pattern to follow is:

1. The starter card if it is a jack (his heels).
2. The play for various combinations - pegging process.
3. The "GO" at the end of pegging.
4. Pone shows his cards and computes scores and records same.
5. The dealer shows, counts and records his hand.
6. Crib is exposed and dealer counts and records its value.

The showing does not include the 31 count or the GO; the only important count that remains is the magic number 15.

CARD VALUES

King, queen, jack, or ten	10
Nine	9
Eight	8
Seven	7
Six	6
Five	5
Four	4
Three	3
Two	2
Ace	1

This point count is only used to determine the number of combinations totaling 15.

Scoring for the Showing

PEG POINTS

His nobs	Jack of the same suit as the starter card	1
Fifteen	Each combination of 15	2
Pairs		2
Triplets	Three of a kind	6
Four of a kind		12
Sequence	Three-card	3
	Four-card	4
	Five-card	5
Flush (dealer and pone)	Four cards in same suit (excluding starter)	4
	Four cards plus starter in same suit	5
Flush (crib)	Four cards in same suit (excluding starter)	0
	Four cards plus starter card in same suit	5

1. The dealer may not interchange cards from the crib with cards from his hand. The crib and the dealer's hand are separate units.
2. The cards of the crib may not be counted as a flush unless the starter card is also of the same suit.
3. His nobs is the jack of the starter's suit when the starter card is not a jack. It is scored during the showing (1 point). His heels is a jack cut as the starter card. It is scored before the play (2 points for the dealer).
4. Each combination adding to 15 is awarded 2 points. Any combinations that differ by one or more cards are considered different.
5. The symbol 15/2 indicates that one 15 combination is

formed for 2 points; 15/4, two combinations; 15/6, for 6
points; and so on to the maximum of 15/16, for 16 points.
6. A card may be included in more than one type of scoring
combination; for example, a queen may be included in a run
as well as in a 15/2 group.

The 15 Count

We begin with a holding, with a king as the starter card,
which contains two combinations of 15.

Hand no. 1:   9-9-6-Q

first	9 + 6 = 15/2
second	9 + 6 = 15/2
pair	9 - 9 = 2
	6 points

Helpful Hints for Counting

You horse racing fans know what it means to box a group of
horses for betting purposes. It is a common way to wager on
the perfecta or the trifecta at the track. For example, the
two most favored horses can be boxed by betting on horses
no. 1-2-3, 1-2-4, 1-2-5, 1-2-6, and so on.

Here is how to box a Cribbage hand made up of the four fives
and a nine-spotter.

Starting at each corner of the rectangle, we combine the
corner five with the five "to the left" and the five "to the
right" for a combination of 15 points. Each of the four

combinations is shown in a triangle of solid lines. (Note that
the nine cannot be used in any combination.)

Announcing the scoring computation for this hand, a player
says: "15/2, 15/4, 15/6, 15/8, plus 12 points for holding four
of a kind" - four fives - "making 20 points to be pegged."

Here is a similar 20-pointer:

                    ♥8

                    ♣8   ♥7 = 15

                    ♠8

                    ♦8

We state it as follows: "15/2, 15/4, 15/6, 15/8, and four eights,
12 points, making a total of 20 points."

Study this hand of three eights, a king, and a seven-spotter:

                    ♥8

        ♠K   ♠8   ♣7 = 15
                    ♦8

There are three 15s made up by combining the seven with
the eight-spotters. There are also the 6 points for the eights
themselves. (The king is useless in this hand.) So we say,
"15/2, 15/4, 15/6, and triplets, making a total of 12."

Note: In figuring the score of a hand, it is easiest to compute
the 15s first and then add on any pairs, triplets, runs and
flushes.

Next we have three sevens, any two of which can be
combined with an ace to make up a 15 combination:

A Lesson in Geometry

The student may visualize the 15/2 combinations of four sevens and an ace from the figure:

There are four small triangles that form 15/2 combinations. Two more 15/2s can be formed by drawing straight lines from corner to corner: 7-A-7 and 7-A-7.

The hand scores 12 holes for the six 15/2 combinations, and 12 more holes for four of a kind.

Runs of Three Can Double Up

A holding may contain a pair as well as two different runs of three cards:

K-♥K-♣Q-♠J-♦9

Analyzing the hand (and ignoring the useless nine) we find:

		POINTS
Run	♥K- ♠Q- ♦J	3
Run	♣K- ♠Q- ♦J	3
Pair	♥K- ♣K	2
		8

A "double run of three" always scores 8 points. When you are counting such a hand you merely state: 'I have a double run for 8," instead of explaining that you have a sequence of three, and another sequence of three, and a pair.

You must learn to count your hand efficiently.

Double Run of Four Scores 10 Points

Take a four-card straight and pair any card:

$$♠4-♥4-♣3-♠2-♠A$$

The player cannot form a 15/2, since the five cards only add up to 14 points. Further analysis shows two sequences, each four cards in length, and a pair of fours:

		POINTS
Run	♥4-♣3-♠2-♣A	4
Run	♠4-♣3-♠2-♣A	4
Pair	♥4-♣4	2
		10

You say: "Double run of four - 10 points." Then record it on the board.

Triple Run Counts 15 Points

This includes a triplet and an overlapping three-card run, e.g.:

$$♦K-♠K-♠K-♣Q-♥J$$

Lets line up the cards to show the three straights:

	POINTS
♦K- ♣Q-♥J	3
♠K-♣Q-♥J	3
♥K-♣Q-♥J	3
Triplet kings	6
	15

Familiarize yourself with the triple run: if there are no 15/
2s and no his nobs, the hand always scores 15.

A Straight That is Quadrupled

Sequences can really get complicated. You will appreciate
the next hand because it scores 16 points in a neat package.
It comes in handy when you want to make a big move
around the corner to Fourth Street:

♠3-♥2-♦2-♠A-♣A

There are two sets of pairs, the aces and the deuces, making
2 x 2 = 4 three-card runs:

	POINTS
♠3-♥2-♣A	3
♠3-♦2-♣A	3
♠3-♥2-♠A	3
♠3-♦2-♠A	3
Two pair	4
	16

First search for the 15/2 possibilities of the hand. (It has
none.) Then shock your opponent by saying: "I have 16
points."

YOUR MEMORY BANK

Learn to associate cards in groups to help you count a hand
quickly.

File these away in your memory bank:

GROUP	READ AS
1-4	5
2-3	5

1-5	6
2-4	6
1-6	7
2-5	7
3-4	7

6-Point Hands

GROUP	READ AS
2-2-3-Q	5-5-10
2-3-3-K	5-5-10
1-1-6-8	7-7-8
2-2-4-9	6-6-9
2-4-4-9	6-6-9

For each of these the count is 15/4 plus a pair, for a score of 6.

Memorizing Some 8-Counters

HAND	COUNT
1-2-3-3	8
1-1-2-3	8
1-2-2-3	8
6-7-8-9	8 (15/4 and a run of four)
10-J-Q-Q	8
10-10-J-Q	8

Count similar combinations of four tenth cards as 8 points.

Try making tables of combinations that yield 10, 12, and 16 points.

You will always be welcome as a player if you can compute combinations rapidly.

A CHEMISTRY TEACHER LEARNS A LESSON

If you are thinking of putting a bragging Cribbage player to the test and deflating his ego, here is how I did it once.

"Joe, come up to the house sometime and I'll show you how to play Cribbage," remarked the chemistry teacher at a Wisconsin high school where I was head football coach some years ago.

"That's my game," continued the test-tube expert. "I know all the hands at a glance, and I know all the tricks of the trade, especially in pegging," my friend with the superiority complex continued.

I thought to myself, "I know how I'll fix him. I'll put him to my special test; and I do hope it works."

So one night when I had no special plans, I casually dropped in on him and he immediately pulled out the board and the deck of cards, saying: "Joe, you'll never forget this night."

I retorted: "I probably won't, and I think that you'll always remember it too."

There was nothing at stake except honor. We split the first two games and he said: "What will you have to drink?" I answered that any kind of soft drink would do and while he was at the refrigerator I took the four fives out of the deck and placed them neatly under the Cribbage board.

Believe it or not, we played five more games and he never missed the five-spotters. I beat him four of those five games and his balloon was apparently punctured.

I thanked him for the enjoyable evening and lifted the Cribbage board to show him the fives, remarking: "You certainly know your Cribbage. You played five games without missing the fives."

I have used this treatment on other braggarts and fortunately, no one has popped me on the jaw. So be careful, and keep your distance with your chin up if you try this stunt.

FLUSHES

Don't count your cards carelessly and miss a flush! Flushes are as important in Cribbage as in Poker. A four-card flush counts 4 points (except for the crib hand), and another point is added if the starter card is of the same suit.

Here is a favorite of mine - a "straight flush" combining a five-card flush and a five-card straight, plus a pair of 15/2s:

8-7-6-5-4 (same suit)

Counting the score:

	POINTS
8-7, combination of 15	2
6-5-4, combination of 15	2
Five-card straight	5
Five-card flush	5
	14

Here are some even higher-scoring hands in which a flush is coupled with other scoring combinations. (The starter card is in another suit in each example.)

FLUSH	STARTER	POINTS
Q-J-10-5	5	21
K-Q-J-5	5	21
8-7-6-1	8	20
7-6-5-4	4	20
6-5-4-3	6	20

FLUSH	STARTER	POINTS
Q-3-2-1	2	18
9-8-7-1	7	18
6-5-4-2	4	18
8-7-6-2	6	18
6-5-4-3	3	18
8-7-6-1	1	17

Other starter cards exist that help the hands listed above.

Discarding Problem

The following common type of hand involves the choice of a straight over a flush with the sacrifice of 1 point.

hearts:	Q-J-6-4
clubs:	10-2

It is before the play, and you do not know the starter card yet. Should you keep the heart flush for 4 points, or should you sacrifice a point and try for a double run by keeping the Q-J-10-2 combination?

Study your position on the board. If 1 point looks very important, hold the flush. A pair, for example, will increase the hand value by a moderate 2 points. But if you are in the mood and position to speculate; hold the run of three. (Discarding will be discussed at length in Chapter IV.)

HIGH-SCORING HANDS

Beginning players may have difficulty in computing the correct values of high-scoring combinations. Therefore, it is a good idea to memorize the following groups.

The 29-Point Perfect Holding

Players holding 29-pointers in sanctioned tournaments receive a plaque for the good fortune along with a cash award. In Grass Roots competition, the luck players receive a Certificate of Merit.

5-5-HN-5-5

The "HN" represents his nobs: the starter card is a five of the same suit as the jack you hold. We compute the scoring carefully:

	POINTS
Jack plus first five	2
Jack plus other three fives (2 each)	6
First, second, third five (sum: 15)	2
First, second, fourth five	2
First, third, fourth five	2
Second, third, fourth five	2
Four of a kind	12
His nobs	1
	29

The odds of being dealt with a 29-point hand in the regular game are 216,580 to 1. For the partnership and five-card game, the mathematicians report that the odds increase to 649,740 to 1.

Millions of players have held four fives, and one of the 16 tenth cards (kings, queens, jacks, and tens), making a hand with a value of 28. That's the 29-pointer without the 1 point for his nobs - which you can't get because you don't hold a jack.

The odds for being dealt a 28 hand are reported to be 15,028 to 1 and in the five-card and partnership contest, the odds increase to 39,506 to 1.

Impossible Scores

One may hear the remark from veteran players: "I have a 19 hand." This is an indication that there isn't a single point in their hand. Other impossible counts are 25, 26 and 27.

Here are 24-Pointers

People turned from five-card Cribbage to the modern six-card variety because the latter has higher-scoring hands. We all enjoy scoring 16, 17, 18, 20, 21, 22, 23, or even 24 - especially when we need a fistful of points to overtake our opponents.

Memorize the following combinations so that when you count your hand you can say, "I have 24 points," without stopping to go through all the calculations.

1-7-7-7-7	4-4-5-6-6
3-3-3-3-9	4-5-5-6-6
3-6-6-6-6	6-7-7-8-8
4-4-4-4-7	7-7-8-8-9
4-4-5-5-6	

Hitting the 23 Mark

This is an unusual score, because there are only two types of combinations which score 23 points:

4-5-5-5-6   5-5-5-HN-J

The 22-Pointer

There are four hands in this classification, made up of three fives and a pair of tenth cards:

5-5-5-K-K	5-5-5-J-J
5-5-5-Q-Q	5-5-5-10-10

Producing 21

Ten of the combinations score 21:

3-3-3-4-5	5-HN-J-J-J
4-4-4-5-6	6-7-7-7-8
4-5-6-6-6	6-7-8-8-8
5-5-5-10-HN	7-7-7-8-9
5-5-HN-J-J	7-8-8-8-9

The Roaring 20s

There are plenty of 20-pointers, especially when you consider that each type can be multiplied by choosing cards
from different suits. This list of pleasing 20-pointers will
give the reader an idea of the possibilities:

1-1-7-7-7	6-6-6-6-9
2-2-2-2-9	6-6-9-9-9
3-3-3-3-6	6-6-7-7-8
3-3-3-9-9	6-6-7-8-8
3-3-4-4-5	6-6-6-9-9
3-3-4-5-5	6-9-9-9-9
3-3-6-6-6	7-7-7-7-8
3-4-4-4-4	7-7-7-8-8
4-4-4-7-7	7-7-8-8-8
5-5-5-5-	7-7-8-9-9
5-5-10-10-10	7-8-8-8-8
5-10-10-10-10	7-8-8-9-9

The combinations with four five range from ace to nine.

The 18-counters (not including ones built on flushes):

3-3-3-6-6	5-5-10-HN-Q
3-6-6-6-9	5-5-HN-Q-K

Some Lucky 17s

2-3-4-4-4	5-5-10-J-Q
3-4-4-4-5	5-5-HN-Q-Q
3-4-5-5-5	6-6-6-7-8
5-5-5-6-7	7-8-9-9-9

Typical "Sweet 16" Hands

Here is a sampling of the relatively common 16-point hands. Mathematicians tell us that there are 160 possible ways to form them. (X indicates a tenth card - ten, jack, queen, or king - that does not pair a card already listed.)

1-6-7-7-8	5-10-10-J-Q
1-6-7-8-8	6-7-7-8-9
2-2-3-3-4	6-7-8-8-9
2-3-3-4-4	8-8-9-9-10
3-3-3-6-9	9-9-10-J-J
3-4-4-5-5	9-10-10-J-J
4-5-5-6-X	10-10-J-J-Q
5-5-6-6-7	10-10-J-Q-Q
5-5-10-10-X	10-J-J-Q-Q
5-5-J-J-X	J-J-Q-Q-K
5-5-Q-Q-X	J-J-Q-K-K
5-5-K-K-X	J-Q-Q-K-K
5-6-6-7-7	

A Few of the 15s

There are 77 possible 15-point combinations, including:

1-1-1-2-3	9-10-J-J-J
1-2-3-3-3	10-10-10-J-Q
5-6-6-6-7	10-J-J-J-Q
8-8-8-9-10	10-J-Q-Q-Q
9-9-9-10-J	J-Q-Q-Q-K
9-10-10-10-J	J-Q-K-K-K

And here are some 14-pointers that turn into 15-point holdings because they include the jack, his nobs, of the turn-up suit:

4-5-5-5-HN	5-9-10-HN-J
5-5-5-6-HN	5-10-10-10-HN
5-5-5-8-HN	5-HN-J-J-Q
5-5-5-9-HN	5-HN-J-J-K
5-5-10-HN-K	

THE MAGIC NUMBER IS 15

Why was the count of 15 set in the pegging process to score 2 points? Why are combinations of the hand-count an objective of scoring? Why was the figure of 31 determined to be the stopping point in pegging? Why was the Go of 34 discarded?

Sir John Suckling, the great gamester, was a keen student of the magic of numbers. In the writer's research of card games, there had been no explanation of why certain numbers were set as goals.

Let's take a look at the single digit numbers of a deck of cards - 9-8-7-6-5-4-3-2-1. Sir John had to be aware of arranging the numbers in a square which when totalled horizontally, vertically, and diagonally add up to 15.

2	7	6	15
9	5	1	15
4	3	8	15
15	15	15	15 15

Every result obtained totals 15. Hence 15 was accepted as

a spot where 2 points are awarded for this accomplishment.

In the matter of the 31-point count for a Go, it was probably derived from the game of Noddy, the forerunner of Cribbage which had the stopping point at 21. The early players of Cribbage determined that 31 should be the Go figure. Cribbage in those days was played with five cards being dealt to each player. In fact, the five-card game is still very popular in England and is considered as a very skilful contest.

With the advent of six cards being dealt to each player and two hands and crib consisting of four cards, the innovators set the Go mark at 34 instead of 31. However, this change failed to gain support and the Go mark remained at 31.

In the United States, Cribbage is played by over 10 million people, principally across the northern states from New England to the shores of the Pacific. It is a favorite in Canada too.

CHAPTER IV

ELEMENTARY STRATEGY

BASICS OF DISCARDING

You will recall that before the starter card is turned, each player discards two of his six cards. The four discards that form the crib, are scored on the dealer's side in the showing.

In general the dealer hopes for a strong crib - but is not eager to make discards that will make him score poorly in the play. The nondealer would also like to hold on to good cards, and hopes he can make the crib weak and unproductive in the showing.

We will discuss the sound principles of discarding two cards. The purpose is to get you new players started and bring you to the point where you really enjoy the game.

Fundamentals

1. Players are guided in the discarding process by the dealer's possession of the crib. You might make one kind of discard when dealer and another when pone. Dealer tends to lay out cards favourable to his crib; his opponent, will try to get rid of cards that have little relationship to each other.

2. Keep in mind that games are won or lost with the discard; hence you must make the best discard possible. Your decision about the layaway should be based on the laws of probability.

3. Whether you lead or trail on the Cribbage board is of great importance; your decisions on throwaways must be sound.

4. Consider also the stage of the game. Being ahead a few pegs on First Street and on Fourth Streeet are two different things.

You may decide to stay even with your opponent on the first three streets and then "play the board" by being conservative - or speculative - as board position dictates near the end of the game.

PONE'S DISCARDS: BALKING THE CRIB

Our cribbage forefathers called contributing two cards with intent to destroy the scoring power of the crib "balking the crib."

Today you may call it busting or killing the crib, but it is still a matter of keeping the dealer from scoring.

Remember that you can keep the dealer from having a 16-point or larger crib but you cannot stop him from counting a 12-pointer.

Give up two cards that on the average will avoid setting up double runs or sequences, triplets and common 15/2 combinations.

A number of players have kept detailed records of 4,000 or even 20,000 cribbage games and find that the average crib is 4.6. For all practical purposes 4.5 points are used by writers and teachers when referring to the value of the crib.

Listed herewith are methods of control that have been effective for years and that should be in the repertoire of every cribbage addict.

1. The best balking card is a king because dealer can only

make a sequence in one direction, downward through the queen and jack. The king is a more effective stopper than the queen.

2. Next to the king, the most effective crib buster is probably an ace, which only makes a sequence upward through the deuce and trey. The drawback is that an ace can be a valuable asset for pegging (in the play).

3. The favorite pairs of busting cards are K-10, K-9, K-8, K-7, K-6, and K-A. A queen may be substituted for the king.

4. Avoid contributing a knave to the dealer's cradle; his "jack-in-the-box" has one chance in four of scoring a point (his nobs), depending on the turn of the starter card.

5. It may not be educationally sound to say it this way, but here are some don'ts.

Don't give an opponent touching cards for his box, and that means K-Q, Q-J, J-10, 10-9, 9-8, 8-7, 7-6, 6-5, 5-4, 4-3, 3-2, or 2-A.

Almost as bad are cards with one space between them: K-J, Q-10, J-9, 10-8, 9-7, 8-6, 7-5, 6-4, 5-3, 4-2, and 3-A. It only takes one card from dealer to form a three-card sequence, and the possibility of a double run is increased.

6. Fear the five-card flush, although the odds against it are high. Other things being equal, pass cards of two different suits to the crib.

7. Try to keep a five-spotter rather than pass it along to your opponent's crib. In general, refrain from discarding an eight or a seven.

8. It may be better to reduce your hand by 2 points rather than make a rich contribution to the box.

9. There are times when you must take a chance of loading up the crib:

8-8-7-7-5-5

Trust to fate, throw caution to the wind and discard the two fives. You must score in order to win and in this instance you must hold on to the 12 points in your hand.

10. To end with a do: Place these wide couplets in the crib without hesitation:

K-10 Q-9 10-4 9-2 8-2

There is no guarantee that you will kill the crib but at least you should limit it to 4, 5, or 6 points.

Recap of defensive discards:

Best Choices	Next Best	Forced
K-9	K-4	9-5
K-10	Q-4	8-5
Q-9	J-A	A-A
K-A	9-A	K-Q
Q-A	8-2	K-K
K-8	7-3	K-2
Q-8	K-7	5-A
K-6	Q-7	5-2
Q-6	8-4	5-3

Consider throwing two cards whose total adds up to an <u>even number</u> as 9 + A instead of 9-2; 8-2 instead of 8-3; 7-3 instead of 7-4; a 10th card and a 4 or 2 instead of 10-3. A throw of 10-4 is safer than 10-2.

Keep odd numbered combinations for pegging 15/2 or 31/2. Two odd cards discarded add up to an even number (9-1 or 7-3) for the crib. The difference is winning or losing.

DEALER'S DISCARDS TO HELP THE CRIB

The crib is your treasure box when you are the dealer. Adjust your tactics accordingly.

1. Throw favourable cards to the crib. Fives are best, then sevens and eights, then sixes and nines.

2. Placing a pair in the crib will often pay large dividends since the possibility of triplets and double runs is increased.

3. Remember there are sixteen tenth cards, almost one-third of the deck.

Cards such as 3-3-2-9 or 4-4-A-7 are excellent to hold on to because of the good probability of cutting a face card or a ten-spotter for the starter, good for a 15/4 with either hand.
For the same reason, a discard of 4-A or 3-2 is good if it agrees with the balance of the hand. (See no.6 below.)

4. Fives are good discards if you don't have picture cards in your hand:

7-5-5-4-A

Throw the two fives into your crib.

5. From a hand composed of high, medium, and low cards, discard the middle cards. This is a common fundamental type of hand:

Q-J-9-7-2-A

Lay out the nine and seven. After the discard your hand looks like this:

Q-J-2-A

The high and low groups you keep present good possibilities

of being combined into 15s. A starter four or three would be wonderful. Then too, the 9-7 is a good foundation for the crib.

6. Cards that add up to 5 are good to keep. Take this hand for example:

K-K-8-4-4-A

Discard a king and the eight. This does not help the crib much, but the 4-4-A, must be kept intact because of the tenth card that may be cut. The chance of turning one of the remaining fourteen tenth cards (you have two kings) is 14 in 46, or 30%.

7. Baiting the crib is sound offensive strategy. Best cards for setting up chances of 15/2s in the crib are:

3-2	5-5	8-7
4-A	6-5	9-6
4-5	5-X	

And don't forget the pairs.

8. Hold on to a run of three cards unless you can score more with another combination. If the starter card builds a double run, the hand goes up by 5 points - from 3 to 8.

9. With a weak hand containing a couple of points or none at all, set your sights on the pegging process. The middle-ranking and low cards are best for the play, so keep them and lay away the tenth cards. This is especially true if you have 5 or 6 points to go to win the game or escape a possible lurch (where pone gets 121 points and you have less than 91 and lose double stakes):

K-J-8-6-4-2

Discard the king and jack.

10. Take the long chance, trying to turn your holding into a juicy winner when you are dangerously behind:

Q-Q-10-10-4-A   discard the 4-A and hope for a jack starter
10-9-6-6-4-4   discard the 10-9 and hope for a five starter

11. Consider keeping an ace or a deuce in a problem hand such as:

K-Q-J-10-9-A

As every Cribbage enthusiast knows, an ace - which is a poor card for the crib - is very helpful in pegging. Discard the king and queen because pone may also throw a king to balk the crib. Using your remaining tenth cards you may be able to bring the count to 31 with your ace.

LAWS OF PROBABILITY

In Cribbage a player is dealt six cards. The other forty-six are unknown - the six in opponents's hand, and the forty left in the deck. One of the unknown cards, the one that is cut for a starter, is a great concern to both players. How can you increase the probability that you will benefit from the as yet unknown starter card?

You can do it by wise discards, based on a sound understanding of the percentages, or odds, in Cribbage. Other things being equal, you want to retain the four cards which benefit from the greatest number of possible starters. If there is only one card that can help the hand you have selected, your chances are only 1 in 46, or 2.2%; but if there are twenty-four such cards, your chances improve to 24 in 46, or 52.2% (see the Expectancy Table. p. 51).

There are, of course, other factors that will influence your discarding decision: What will the effect of your discard be on the crib? What is your position on the board? Are you ahead or behind your adversary and by how much? Do you need to take chances or should you make conservative and balking discards? But always remember that in games involving an element of chance, the successful players are those who have a system - those who play the percentages.

Let's look at a simple example. If you hold 9-9-7-7, how many favorable starters are there? Assume that you have discarded a six and a king.

This hand is already good for 4 holes - the two pairs. With a cut of an eight, the hand explodes into a 20-pointer! Among the forty-six unknown cards there are four eights. What are the odds of drawing one of them? Answer: 4 in 46, or 8.7%, or 10.50 to 1 odds against.

But there are several other cards which will also garner points:

	CHANCES
Ace adds 2 points	4
Six adds 4 points	3
Seven adds 4 points	2
Nine adds 4 points	2

(There are only three sixes left - you discarded one.) Altogether there are 15 chances to improve the hand with the starter card: four eights, four aces, three sixes, two sevens, and two nines. What are the odds of drawing one of these cards? Answer: 15 in 46, or 32.6%, or 2.07 to 1 against.
To help you answer such questions I have prepared the following table. The table is as simple and understandable as possible, so that you can refer to it during a game or even memorize a few key lines with little effort.

Wergin's Expectancy Table

Favorable Cards	Unfavorable Cards	Odds Against You	Percentage In Your Favor
24	22	0.92/1	52.2
23	23	1.00/1	50.0
22	24	1.09/1	47.8
21	25	1.19/1	45.7
20	26	1.30/1	43.5
19	27	1.42/1	41.3
18	28	1.56/1	39.1
17	29	1.71/1	37.0
16	30	1.88/1	34.8
15	31	2.07/1	32.6
14	32	2.29/1	30.4
13	33	2.54/1	28.3
12	34	2.83/1	26.1
11	35	3.18/1	23.9
10	36	3.60/1	21.7
9	37	4.11/1	19.6
8	38	4.75/1	17.4
7	39	5.57/1	15.2
6	40	6.67/1	13.0
5	41	8.20/1	10.9
4	42	10.50/1	8.7
3	43	14.33/1	6.5
2	44	22.00/1	4.3
1	45	45.00/1	2.2

Check the two answers given above with the table.

The lower the odds are against you and the higher the percentage of events in your favour, the better your chances are of drawing a helpful card.

Apply Logic

The answer to many discarding problems can be found right in front of you - on the cribbage board. You must play the board!

Are you ahead, or are you trailing, and by how much? Is it your last chance to speculate and try for the big score? Note that some players always "shoot the works" rather than take the sensible approach. They are losing players in the long run.

Let's discuss a riskier discard from our sample hand. We began with 9-9-7-7-6-K and discarded 6-K. Now, what if we retained 9-9-7-6 and discarded the king and a seven, still a good balking throwaway?

The new hand is already good for 6 points, a 2-point improvement over 9-9-7-7 and it has a bright future, since possible starting cards are:

AVAILABLE	POINT INCREASE	TOTAL POINTS
Two nines	6	12
Four eights	10	16
Three sixes	6	12

There are nine desirable cards which will at least double the original count from 6 to 12 holes. The odds of hitting one of them is 19.6%; of cutting an eight-spotter, only 8.7%

Here are several more sample hands, where you must decide which card to discard. Practice using the Expectancy Table, and you will develop a scientific approach to Cribbage.

Hand no. 1: Devotees are continually faced with the choice of discarding a pair and holding a three-card straight, or breaking up the straight by laying away two cards from it:

Q-Q-10-9-8-5

Three of the sixteen tenth cards in the deck are in your hand, leaving thirteen among the unknowns. There are also three fives to add to your list of desirables.

I recommend that the 9-8 be discarded, leaving:

Q-Q-10-5

This hand - already an 8-pointer - has a good percentage opportunity to go places. There are sixteen helping cards:

	POINT INCREASE	TOTAL POINTS
Four kings	2	20
Two queens	6	14
Four jacks	8	16
Three tens	4	12
Three fives	8	16

The Expectancy Table shows that the odds are less than 2 - 1 against, namely 34.8%, that one of the sixteen cards will be turned by the dealer for the starter. Not bad!

Hand no. 2: Shooting for a double run is not always the best policy because the 15/2 combinations may bring the best results.

Q-J-10-7-3-2

A discard of 2-7 or 3-7 doesn't offer the greatest potential for the hand; a cut for a double run of the tenth cards produces a final count of 8 or 9 holes 28.3% of the time.

Look a little farther, because the 15/2s can bring juicier
scores. Here's how the hand will look if you lay out the Q-7,
a balking combination;

J-10-3-2

Here are the chances of improvement - all thirty-five of
them!

	POINT INCREASE	TOTAL POINTS
Four kings	2	6
Three queens	5	9
Three jacks	4	8
Three tens	4	8
Four nines	3	7
Four fives	4	8
Four fours	3	7
Three treys	6	10
Three deuces	6	10
Four aces	3	7

Now we have 8, 9, or 10 holes 41.3% of the time; the lesser
improvements are also more probable, and even without
any improvements the hand is a point better.

Hand no. 3: This illustration is particularly interesting: it
involves the apparent sacrifice of 4 holes. The sacrifice will
pay off in the long run, however, by almost 1 hole:

6-6-3-3-2-2

If you discard the 6-6 and retain 3-3-2-2, you have 4 points
already and the starter card will improve the average scoring of the hand to 10.26 (every cut except six helps). But if
you discard the deuces and hold 6-6-3-3, the hand, which
gives you 8 points to begin with instead of 4, will average
9.48 holes, and only a three, six, or nine will be a useful
starter card.

A complete analysis shows how 3-3-2-2- is better:

	POINT INCREASE	TOTAL POINTS
Four kings	8	12
Four queens	8	12
Four jacks	8	12
Four tens	8	12
Four nines	2	6
Four eights	4	8
Four sevens	4	8
Two sixes	0	4
Four fives	2	6
Four fours	12	16
Two treys	4	8
Two deuces	4	8
Four aces	12	16

Of every forty-six hands based on 3-3-2-2, on the average, two will score 4 points; eight, 6 points; twelve, 8 points; sixteen, 12 points; and eight, 16 points. Total score for forty-six hands is 472 points, or 10.26 per hand. (You began with 4 points and added an average of 6.26 points.)

But if you keep 6-6-3-3, beginning with 8 points, you will improve by an average of only 1.48 points, leaving you with only 9.48. Of forty-six hands, thirty-eight will still have only 8 points; four (nines) will have 14 points; two (sixes) will have 20 points; and two (treys) will have 18 points. Total, 436 points for forty-six hands.

It should be added that with the better choice you give a pair of sixes to the crib; with the inferior choice the crib gets a pair of deuces. Whether you are dealer or pone, there is not much difference what the pair is, either in your play or the crib's showing.

The purpose of this discussion on percentages is to make you a thinking player with a system to follow in making your decisions.

In the future you will be applying logic in selecting discards based upon board position as well as the favorable and unfavorable percentages. Good luck!

DISCARDING TO YOUR OWN CRIB

Best Cards	Single Gap	Touching Cards	Pairs
5-5	A-3	A-2	A-A
10-5	2-4	2-3	2-2
9-6	4-6	3-4	3-3
8-7	6-8	4-5	4-4
8-A	7-9	5-6	5-5
7-A	9-J	6-7	6-6
6-4	10-Q	7-8	7-7
6-A	J-K	8-9	8-8
4-3		9-10	9-9
4-A		10-J	10-10
3-2		J-Q	J-J
		Q-K	Q-Q
			K-K

DEFENSIVE STRATEGY

Defensive strategy usually refers to the player who has fewer points on the board - not to the pone defending against the dealer.

Athletic coaches say, "Defense you always have with you. A team may have an off night and have trouble scoring, but the defense will keep it in the game."

The same is true of Cribbage. If the opposition is drawing excellent cards and is blessed with lucky starter cards, you must do your utmost to control the pegging and the crib to eliminate the possibility of being skunked or left in the lurch.

Some sound defensive tactics are presented so that you may advance in knowledge and eventually receive a master's degree in Cribbage.

When play begins, your first objective is to get some 15/2s. If you can't, you must try to prevent your opponent from making a 15/2 - which is the same gain in score for you, really, as making one yourself.

Your second objective is to run the count to 31 for 2 points, or at least get a 1-point Go. If luck doesn't favour you, why not gain a point by forcing your opponent to fall short of 31 so he gets a 1-point Go instead of a 2-point Go?

In the defensive maneuvers presented below, you will note some overlapping of offense and defense, because your countermoves, with luck, may not only keep your opponent from pegging but result in your pegging instead.

1. *Playing Off*

This action is the opposite of playing on (where you encourage opponent to begin a sequence). Leave enough of a gap between the first card played by pone and your card to eliminate the possibiity of a sequence.

Pone leads a nine and you counter with a queen (rather than a jack), making the count 19. The gap of two cards between nine and queen is too large for him to fill in a straight. Keep aware of playing wide, thus defending against runs.

2. *Beware of Pairs*

When your adversary leads in a two-handed game, defensive player avoids or is wary of pairing his card which may be his bait for making a triplet.

If opponent has played a card making 15 and scoring 2 points, you are reasonably safe in pairing his card, unless he played a six or an eight. Your six brings the count to the dangerous 21 mark (any tenth card gives him 2 points for Go). Your eight sets him up for 8 points if he holds the third eight.

3. *Triplets*

You often have the choice of making 2 points by pairing pone's leadoff card or by scoring on a 15.2. 'Tis better to make the 15/2 than to allow pone to make triplets and score 6 points!.

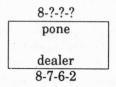

Pone leads his eight. Dealer is safer to play the seven than the eight.

4. *Split a Pair of Fives*

Don't get into a position where you must lead a five from a pair of these precious cards, thus giving up points.

Holding 9-6-5-5, play a five early, when convenient; otherwise your first five may be the start of the second series of play, after a Go.

5. *Stay off Thin Ice*

Running the count to 21 can get you a cold bath when

adversary responds with a roaring "31 for 2 holes."

Tenth cards are plentiful in the deck. There are sixteen of them.

6. *The Safest Card to Lead*

The reader keeps hearing a monotonous "Don't do this and don't do that. Don't lead this card, and better not lead the other one."

Well, what should you lead?
Solve the problem by leading a four-spotter.

Most writers have indicated that a four is the best defensive lead because the dealer is unable to make an immediate 15/2. It is better to save the other small, safe cards -the aces. deuces, and treys - for making 15, a Go, or even 31.

A tenth card is a relatively safe lead if you have no four-spotter. The high card lets you save low cards for when you may need them.

7. *Don't Get Behind the Eight Ball*

Take preventive measures with responding cards. As dealer, don't set up the count so that pone can make 4 holes.

After a seven has been led, avoid taking the count to 11 with a four-spotter. Pone may have another four and by hitting the count at 15, he scores double - 2 for the pair and 2 for the 15.

The same is true if the count is 23. Avoid playing a four, upping the total to 27, because there is a possibility of pone scoring 4 holes if he holds another four.

There are other cards that place a person behind the eight

ball. Don't make 28 with a trey, 13 with a deuce, 22 with a nine, 26 with a five, 24 with a seven, 23 with an eight, or 21 with a tenth card. If pone matches your last card, he will score double.

8. *The Equalizer*

With a nine and a three in the hand, an equalizer play will delay the decision of the game. You are pone:

```
            9-3-?-?
         ┌─────────────┐
         │   pone      │
         │             │
         │   dealer    │
         └─────────────┘
            3-?-?-?
```

Start with the three and if dealer goes for the pair, counter with the nine, evening the score with a 15/2.

The same principle applies if you hold a four and a seven. Open with the four and if dealer racks up 2 points for a pair, equalize by playing the seven.

9. *The World's Worst Lead*

Of course, there must be an opening lead that is stupid, silly, foolish, and irrational. For obvious reasons, the world's worst opening lead is a five-spotter.

Charity begins at home - not over a Cribbage board.

10. *Avoid the 16 Count*

It's unsafe to take the running count to 16 unless you are sure you can play another card (holding a five or lower);

Q-J-10-5

```
┌─────────────────┐
│ pone            │
│                 │
│ dealer          │
└─────────────────┘
```

9-8-7-6

Pone led the jack and dealer countered with the six, saying, "16." Pone moved the count to 26 with his ten-spotter.

Dealer had to pass and pone played his five for 31 and 2 points.

Correct play: J-8-10 for 28; pone's play of the five for 31 is prevented.

11. *Don't Throw a Boomerang*

Leads of sevens and eights are dangerous; they often come back to haunt you or knock you out. Take this hand:

8-8-7-7

```
┌─────────────────┐
│ pone            │
│                 │
│ dealer          │
└─────────────────┘
```

8-7-7-A
or
8-8-7-7

There is only one sensible lead to avoid getting hit with the Australian flying object; an eight, because four eights are an unplayable 32, while four sevens are 28 and net dealer 12 points for quadruplets and an extra point for Go.

If the dealer holds 8-8-7-7, 8-7-7-A, or a similar combination, a seven starts a fateful series. Dealer scores on a pair, pone cashes the third seven for triplets and 6 points, and dealer comes roaring down the stretch with the fourth seven for 12 points - and the Go makes it 13.

Yes, these hands do happen and they always seem to occur down on Fourth Street.

ELEMENTARY PEGGING STRATEGY

Games are usually won or lost in the pegging process! Many basketball coaches maintain that a good offense is the best defense. The same is true of the play in Cribbage. Approach the game aggressively, positively, and be prepared to attack with the four cards of your hand.

Because the circle of opponents is limited, active players usually have a daily one-on-one confrontation with a member of the family or someone down at the club or pub. Always be ready to make an illogical play and upset the routine. Put a little spice into the contest. Vary your plays and surprise the opponent.

Pone has opportunities to maneuver pegging points. Here are some tricks of the trade.

1. *The Sucker Play*

If you hold a deuce and a trey, start the attack by leading the three, often dealer will take the bait and respond with a tenth card, making the count 13. The deuce hits 15 and you peg 2 points immediately.

By the same token, holding a 4-A, open with the four and if pone pushes the count up to 14, the ace brings home 2 points.

The above procedure also tends to prevent the establishment of sequences.

2. *Bait the Hook!*

To lead from a pair is a standard opening play. If the dealer makes a pair, then counter by lining up three of a kind for 6 holes.

Rarely will the dealer spoil your day by playing the fourth card for 12 points.

But don't lead from a pair of fives; a tenth card makes 15/2. If you have a pair, avoid starting the attack with one of them; opponent has been tricked before and will shy away from making a pair. Select a higher card for the first play, later, play from the pair. It has a better chance to net you triplets after the 15 count has been reached:

```
            10-9-2-2
         ┌──────────────┐
         │    pone      │
         │              │
         │    dealer    │
         └──────────────┘
            8-7-6-2
```

Pone opens the nine and if dealer brings the count to 15, slip a deuce out, making the count 17. Now, if dealer holds a two he feels safe in pairing. Pone retaliates with the third deuce for 6 points.

3. *An Ounce of Prevention is Worth a Pound of Cure*

If you hold a 9-6 couplet, there is an excellent reason for playing the six rather than the nine.

Lead the six, and if dealer responds with a nine for 15/2, counter with your nine, scoring 2 for a pair and bringing the running score to 24. Now dealer cannot make triplets without going over 31.

If you had opened the nine, and dealer hit 15/2 with a six, your pairing the six would move the running score to 21, to the advantage of the dealer - who slams the door at 31 with a tenth card or takes 6 holes with a six, scoring 4 or 9 holes against 2 for you.

4. *Hit the Bull's-eye of 31*

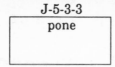

J-5-3-3

pone

If you open the play with a three, dealer's most common play is to jump the count to 13 with a tenth card. If it is a jack, pair it. Otherwise move the count to 16 with your remaining three-spotter.

Another tenth card from dealer will advance the count to the 26-mark, you've been waiting for, and your five hits 31 for 2 pegging points.

5. *Lead the Middle Card*

When you have to lead from a sequence of three cards start with the middle card:

J-10-9-5

pone

Play the ten and you can go up or down to form a sequence.

From 8-7-6 lead the seven; if dealer goes for the 15/2, counter with the six for a three-card sequence and rack up 3 points.

6. *Picture Cards*

What should be led from the following?

K-Q-J-5
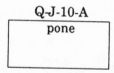

The queen. Assume, for example, that dealer holds four tenth cards. By leading the queen you have him hooked for 3 points for a sequence of three tenth cards and a 1-point go at 30 for you. If you lead the king, dealer can play off with a ten-spotter, conceding you the 1-point go but depriving you of the 3-point straight.

Either way, dealer must start a new series, and your counter of a five nets a 15/2.

7. *Use Your Ace*

Holding this hand:

Q-J-10-A

Lead the ten, luring dealer on with the opportunity of avoiding a sequence by playing his king. Counter with the queen or jack to bring the count to 30, and if he lacks an ace, score 2 with your ace.

8. *Risky Business*

Yes, going into business is risky, but we mean that a player must be aware of the risks when sevens and eights are being played.

It can pay dividends, all the same, to lead out one of them if you have something to back up your play:

8-7-7-A

The aggressive play is to lead a seven and if dealer replies 15/2 with an eight, counter with your eight for a pair, making the count 23. If dealer responds with a seven instead of an eight, you can drill 6 holes with triplets.

In opening with a seven, you are "thinking positive" in that you don't expect him to hold a pair of sevens. If he does....well, it's a risky business!

The next illustrations demonstrate countermoves that dealer can use in combating the plays of pone.

9. *Jackpot!*

On occasion, dealer may encourage pone to form a sequence which will pay dividends on either the sixth or seventh card:

Q-7-6-3

pone
dealer

5-4-2-A

On pone's opening play of a seven, respond with a five, allowing adversary to complete a three-card sequence with his six-spotter. Then retaliate with your four, scoring on a four-card straight.

Now if pone extends the run to five cards with a three, stretch the straight to six cards with your deuce and, of course, put the frosting on the cake with your ace, making the running count 28. Take 8 holes--1 for the Go and 7 for the run. Net results of this series is pone 8, dealer 18.

10. *Playing On*

This means playing a card that encourages the formation of

a straight. If adversary leads a four, play a deuce, encouraging him to construct a three-card straight.

Of course you must be able to back up your play with an ace or a five if adversary plays a trey.

11. *Setting a Trap*

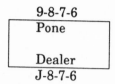

9-8-7-6

Pone

Dealer

J-8-7-6

Players favor the lead of the 8-spot ter in this and similar hands.

One reliable stunt in the dealer's bag of tricks is playing a 7 on pone's 8 for a 15/2 score. Pone immediately retaliates with the 9 for a run of three--3 points.

With the count at 24, dealer seals the play with a 6, for a run of four and the Go, netting a total of 7 points--2 for 15/2, run for 4, and Go. Pone is outscored 7 to 3.

Second Series:

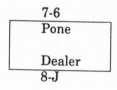

7-6

Pone

Dealer

8-J

In the second series pone favors the lead of the 7, dealer makes it a 15/2 with an 8 and marks up 2 holes. Pone responds with the 6 for 3 holes and a count of 21.

Dealer finishes the series by hitting 31/2 with the jack. Pone scored 3 holes while dealer netted 4. On the complete hand pone scored 6 and the dealer 11.

Dealer had the opportunity of making a super play in the

second series by refusing the 15/2 when pone led the 7.

A better play at the time was the jack making the count 17. Pone's 6 would make the total 23 and dealer's 8 would hit 31/2, outscoring pone 2 to 0.

THE COUNT OF 11

After the first lead, a responding card that brings the total to 11 upsets pone's pegging strategy.

When a deuce is led, a play of a 9 makes the count 11 and blocks off opponent's original plan. Pone is hoping for a 15/2 with the play of a tenth card by the opponent. Pone doesn't dare to make the count 21 with a tenth card.

Thus, pone is forced to make an undesired play when switching to defense.

The same applies for the opening of a 3 or a 4. Dealer should make the count 11 if possible. When a 7 is played to a 4, average players stop and wonder what dealer is up to. As a 7 is a card of special value, opponents do not dare to pair it, much less play a card that will produce a run above the 7 or below it.

If the hand calls for it, play an ace on the lead of a tenth card to hit 11.

Making the count 11 is a maneuver that puts the opponent on defense and restricts options for the next play.

THREES, SIXES, AND NINES CONFUSE SOME PEOPLE

Many average players experience difficulty in counting hands that include the 3's, 6's, and 9's. To make it easier for these people, the simple ways will be demonstrated herewith.

The 24-point hands, containing four-of-a-kind, are easy to count when boxed.

```
┌─────────────┐      ┌─────────────┐
│ 3         3 │      │ 6         6 │
│      9      │      │      3      │
│ 3         3 │      │ 6         6 │
└─────────────┘      └─────────────┘
```

All the other hands of lesser value are charted below.

Figure the 15/2's on each side of the box using the 9 with each pair of 3's, and then criss-cross the 9 with the corners. It all adds up to 15/12. Then add 12 points for having four 3/s, making a 24-point hand.

Then use the same process in the combination of the 3 with the four 6's.

Simple, isn't it?

Charts of other high scoring hands including the 9's, 6's, and 3's

20-Point Hands

6--6--6--6--9	9--9--9--9--6	3--3--3--3--6
3--3--6--6--6	3--3--3--9--9	6--6--9--9--9
	6--6--6--9--9	

18 Point Hands
3--3--3--6--6   3--6--6--6--9

16-Point Hand
3--3--3--6--9

14-Point Hand
3--3--6--6--9

12 Point Hand
3--3--6--9--9
3--6--9--9--9

When a cribbage business card was printed with some of the difficult counting combinations on the rear side, not only did players keep the card, but they asked for several more cards.

3-3-3-3 + 6 = 20	4-4-5-5 + 6 = 24
3-3-3-3 + 9 = 24	4-5-5-5 + 6 = 23
3-3-3-6 + 6 = 18	5-5-5-5 + 6 = 20
3-3-3-9 + 9 = 20	6-6-6-3 + 9 + 18
3-3-3-6 + 9 = 16	6-6-6-6 + 3 = 24
3-3-3-4 + 5 = 21	6-6-6-3 + 3 = 20
3-3-4-4 + 5 = 20	7-7-7-7 + 1 = 24

HOW TO BECOME A POPULAR CRIBBAGE PLAYER

Cribbage players should complete a game in 12 to 15 minutes. The one thing that players dislike is a slow player. If you want to impress your opponents, learn how to count your hand quickly. If you can keep the game moving at a steady pace, you will be welcomed by veteran players.

Let's get started right away in memorizing certain groups of hands. By now, you know that a double run scores 8 points. Add this hand to your memory: 9-8-7-6 always scores 8 points so don't bother counting it out, just say: "I have eight" and peg 8 points.

Hands that always score 12 points:

A pair of face cards and two 5's, K-K-5-5, or combinations of

9-9-6-6	8-8-7-7
Q-Q-4-4-A	J-J-3-3-2

Triplets with three 15/2 combinations are also on the 12-point list:

10-10-10-5	9-9-9-6	8-8-8-7
	6-6-6-9	7-7-7-8

Don't count these out saying: "15/2, 15/4, 15/5 and triplets for 6; 6 and 6 are 12". Merely say: "Twelve" and peg the 12 points.

Sixteen Pointers

Let's put a couple of 16-point hands in our memory bank. For instance: with the 9-8-7-6 hand that counts 8 points, if the starter matches one of them, the hand increases to 16. There are three combinations of 15/2 plus two runs of four which are always good for ten points.

Avoid counting out: 9-6-6-6 and K-K-K-5

Merely say: 15/6 and 6 is 12.

How to Eliminate Other Delays

<u>Shuffling:</u> Riffle the pack twice and do about two over and unders and then place pack for your opponent to cut. Don't shuffle, shuffle, and talk because you are wasting time. If you can play a game in 15 minutes, you will have played four in one hour. On the other hand, if it takes you 20 minutes to play a game, you only play three in an hour.

<u>Gathering the Cards</u>: When you are the next dealer, take your counted hand, push the starter card off the pack, and take the pack with your counted hand and start shuffling while opponent is counting the hand and the crib. Keep the game moving!

<u>Discarding</u>: If there is only one logical discard, make it promptly. With a lot of practice, a person can make the ordinary discards without delay.

<u>Playing</u>: Plan your plays ahead. If there is only one play to make, make it. Studying it will not change the cards. Some people hesitate to make a play when they have a pair to choose from.

<u>Post Mortems</u>: Included are discussions such as: "If I had another ace, I would have pegged four points. If I would have cut a five, I would have won." Forget the "ifs" and move to the next hand.

A Homework Assignment.....

HOW TO PLAY CRIBBAGE SOLITAIRE

Crib enthusiasts have invented a number of solitaire games based upon cribbage. In the author's estimation the following is the best. Frequently, a person has a sleepless night and why not get up and forget the cares of the world with 30 or 40 solitaire games?

Solitaire means, of course, to play alone. This mental exercise is taught to our children to help them count cribbage points more quickly. And slow players are told to use this activity to recognize scoring values more rapidly.

The four cards are dealt off the top of the pack and laid, face up, across the table as in the diagram. Spaces 1 to 4 are used

to start with. One card is laid aside to build the crib of four
cards.

HANDS

	A	B	C	D	

Place 1st to 4th
card here...
Place 6th to 9th
card here.....

11th card to 14th
here.....
Place 16th to 19th

here.....

5th card is crib
card and goes here face down

10th card here

CRIB

15th card here

20th card here

It is to be remembered that starting with the sixth card, it
is turned face up and after a little study, a person places it
where it fits with a previous card. Decide where it should
be placed under Hand A, B, C, or D.

For example, if the sixth card is a five-spotter, place it under
another five or a face card, or even a six or a four. A five
works good in building a high scoring hand. Try to make the
best cribbage hands possible. Once a card is placed, it must
stay in that spot.

The sixth to ninth cards may be placed anywhere in their
row. The same thing is done with cards eleventh to
fourteenth. It must be remembered to keep cards in their
own row across. Repeat the process for the last row and the
crib.

Next, cut the pack and turn up a Starter Card. Take Hand
A of four cards with the starter, count the cribbage points.

Write the total down on paper or advance that number of holes on the cribbage board.

Then repeat the process for Hands B, C, and D, and finally the crib. Total the hands and crib together for the final score. A count of 32 is considered the average or the par score.

This solitary exercise is excellent practice as a person has the opportunity of counting five hands. As it doesn't take much time, many hands may be played in an hour's time.

To be a popular player, one must be able to recognize the scoring combinations and to count the points rapidly.

HOW 20 POINTS MAY BE PEGGED IN ONE SERIES

Many times during one's career, a hand may be held in which it is possible to peg 20 holes in a single series. Of course the opponent, the pone in this example, must have a combination of cards that fits the pattern.

Every Knight of the Peg should be aware of the requirements and keep the hand in the bag of tricks, hoping for its appearance. It may come at a lucrative tournament when a person's pegs come from nowhere and end up in the game hole.

There are many possibilities of pone's hand containing the necessary ingredients

```
            K-Q-J-A
         ┌──────────┐
         │   pone   │
         │          │
         │  dealer  │
         └──────────┘
            7-A-A-A
```

Pone opened his with queen for a count of 10. The dealer

responded with his seven and pone retaliated with his king; now the count stood at 27.

Dealer continued with an ace, making the total 28, and pone's ace made it 29 and 2 points for the pair.

Dealer pegged six points for triplets with the third ace, making the count 30. Pone passed, and dealer played the fourth ace, scoring 12 for four of a kind. In addition, he finished on 31, so the go was worth 2 points.

Dealer scored:	POINTS
Triplets	6
Quadruplets	12
Go	2
	20

This scribe has held 7-A-A-A and brought it to a successful conclusion. Many times the combination has been held, but the opposition did not co-operate.

It is hoped that this elusive hand will return more often than Halley's comet.

PEGGING 29 OR 30 POINTS FOR TOPS

These rare scores are recorded when the two players hold identical hands of two sets of low cards, 4's down to the aces. The dealer scores 29 holes while pone makes 12 holes.,

4-4-3-3
Pone

Dealer
4-4-3-3

If the 4's are played first, dealer scores 2 for pairing and takes 12 more for quadruplets, a total of 14. In the meantime, pone cashes 6 points for triplets.

Following this routine, the 3's are played with the same results except that dealer adds 1 point for the Go. Dealer's scoring adds up to 29.

LETS GO ONE BETTER AND PEG 30 POINTS

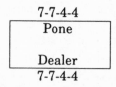

7-7-4-4

By playing the 7's first there is a Go at 28 on the first series. And, of course, there is a Go when the final 4 is played. The dealer scores 15 points on each series (2-12-1) for a hand total of 30 peg points.

RAGGEDY ANN

Special mention is made of the following hand, because average players continually miscount it.

6-7-8-A-A

It is called Raggedy Ann because the ragamuffin doll was loved, chewed upon by the dog, and booted into every corner of a house. Cribbage players boot it every day.

Can you count the straight and the 15's to score 13 points? Many people count it 11.

Raggedy Ann has a brother called Raggedy Andy. The hand consists of 6-7-8-2-2 for 11 holes.

Do not play a six on a four or vice versa, because opponent's five spotter totals 15, scoring 5 holes.

Reference by Gayton to "Noddy boards" in 1654 implies that a board was used for scoring.

All evens do not a 15/2 make!

David Parlett draws attention to the rhythmic jingles that are a part of Cribbage: "Anyone unfortunate enough to bring the count to twenty-one cannot but cringe in anticipation of 'his opponent's rhyming cry, when he slaps down a ten, 'and now you're done."

> *22--and nine will do*
> *23--and eight's a spree*
> *24--and seven's a score*
> *25--and six alive*
> *27--and four's Tw'eleven*
> *28--and three's just great*
> *29--and two's just fine*
> *31--and now you're done*

Parlett continues by asking: "What has become of the language that has given us his nobs, his nibs, his heels, muggins, peggin out, in the lurch, how's that for starters, what a turn up and any old irons?"

Cribbage is fun because:
1. It relieves tension
2. It does not require"card sense"
3. It requires only a knowledge of simple arithmetic
4. It affords the opportunity of applying simple logic.

Have you ever met "the goose", the person who is always stretching his neck to get a peek at your hand? Hold your cards close to your chest, since "one peek is worth two finesses."

They always say: "Closeness only counts in Horseshoes." Apparently gamesters have overlooked the fact that closeness counts in Cribbage, since getting close to a 31 count, scores 1 hole for a Go. Let's say: "Closeness only counts in Horseshoes and Cribbage."

The average number of holes to be made in the pegging on each deal is 4 to 5. The dealer has the advantage because he plays the last card, which quarantees him 1 hole.

The appeal of Cribbage is evident from two facts:
1. There have been relatively few changes made in the original game.

2. It remains after more than three centuries as one of the most popular card games.

CHAPTER V

CRIBBING ALONG WITH THE MASTERS

Aim for the Last Hole

Maneuvers which facilitate your getting a Go:

Holding two low cards and two high cards, lead from the former.

Example: K-Q-3-2. Lead the deuce or trey.

Holding one low card and three high cards, lead from the latter (other things being equal).

Suppose as dealer you hold a ten and a five to start the second series of pegging, and you need two holes to win the game. Lead the ten in the hope that your adversary makes a 15/2; then you can retaliate by pairing his five.

Play the Averages

Situation 1: As dealer you need 3 to 5 points to win the game, while pone needs 7 to 8, or even 6 points. You know that you must peg out during the play to win.

Break up your medium or high pairs and hold pegging cards. thus retaining four cards in your hand that may pair your opponent, keeping a better chance of making a 15/2 or 31:

```
┌─────────────┐
│             │
│             │
│   dealer    │
└─────────────┘
   Q-9-9-7-5-2
```

Discard the Q-9 to the crib, because the game will be over before the crib is counted. Retain the 9-7-5-2. If any of the following cards is led by pone, you can peg 2 holes: K-Q-J-10-9-8-7-6-5-2.

If you discard the 2-7 and keep 4 points in your hand (Q-5-9-9) you may never have the chance to count them.
You can peg 2 holes on seven of pone's possible ranks (K-Q-J-10-9-6-5), compared to ten ranks listed above.

Situation 2: With the same score, you hold two pairs:

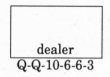

dealer
Q-Q-10-6-6-3

Throw the Q-6 couplet to the crib, and you can peg on leads of Q-10-9-6-5-3.

If you discard the 10-3, keeping Q-Q-6-6 with its 4 points, you won't have time to show and score, the possibilities for pegging are reduced by two denominations, to Q-9-6-5.

The Loser Deals

In multi-matches the loser of a game makes the first deal of the next game. The American Cribbage Congress decided that this was the only fair method.

Of course, the cut of the pack determines the dealer of the first game.

There is one exception to this rule. In tournaments where players are scheduled to meet an opponent in two games of a qualifying round, each contestant has a turn at starting one of the games.

Favor the Crib

Some dealers tend to favor the crib over their own hand when deciding on a discard, because there are more chances to improve the crib after dealer's discard, with the two cards thrown by the pone and the starter card.

This practice is more valid for the five-card contest than for the six-card game. Think about it!

Have a Game Plan

As dealer for the start of the game, it appears that players are equal. But they are not. Because of having the crib, the dealer has a seven-point advantage.

Pone must be aggressive to make up the disadvantage while dealer should control pone's pegging.

With the start of the second deal, note the relative scores on the board and play on or off accordingly.

You may have to change strategy radically if you go way ahead or fall far behind.

If you trail and you pick up some interesting cards that may help you catch up, play for a lucky cut, which may really put you back in the ball game:

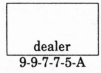

dealer
9-9-7-7-5-A

Berkely, describing six-card Cribbage in his 1901 monograph, referred to the skill and scientific arrangement of this English game.

Discard the 5-A and hope for a lucky eight starter, rather than discarding the sevens.

If your cards are bad and there is little prospect of improving your position, try to keep your opponents from scoring. Stall until the next hand.

HOT AND COLD DECKS

Every cardplayer has encountered the superstitious individual who keeps wanting to change decks because the cards are "cold". There is some wisdom in his superstition.

It has been noted that a deck becomes cold because of artificial patterns formed from playing and (often none too thorough) shuffling. Some people naturally deal out low-scoring hands because of the type of shuffle that they employ. This theory is subscribed to by a number of expert Cribbage players.

Other Cribbage fanatics deal high-scoring hands consistently, because with the method of shuffling and perhaps play of the cards, patterns are formed and continuously repeated, shuffle after shuffle. Experts agree with this statement too.

If the cards were dealt in a truly random manner, no such patterns could be predicted, although hot and cold streaks would still appear.

Freak Hands Are Interesting

The most exciting hands are the freak high-scoring combinations, or those with abnormal distribution. It has been noticed that when one player's holding is unusual, the adversary probably has an odd hand too.

In a three-handed game, also, with the usual nonrandom shuffling, when one player holds only 2 points in his hand, the two competitors tend to score a couple of points or so.

The Hot Deck

A "hot" deck is one in which 12-point hands are common and 20-pointers are far from rare. The deck may stay hot for four or five games, but, alas, the lucky cards may favor only your opponent.

Change Decks

If the cards are cold for you, by all means try another deck for the next game. It is your perogative. However, the change is not permitted during a game.

If your scoring doesn't change with a second deck, then try a third one, and if there is still no improvement, terminate play and reread this book. There must be something else wrong.

COMMON SENSE

Webster offers the following definition for the word "psychology";

   a. the science dealing with the mind and with mental and emotional processes.
   b. the science of human behavior.
   c. the sum of the actions, traits, attitudes, thoughts, and mental states of a person.

I prefer a simpler definition: the application of pure common sense to a given situation.

There is lot more to the science of Cribbage than just

discarding two cards, turning a starter card, and going through the routine of counting 15/2 and run of three. You must be aware of your opponent's mental processes, baehavior, attitudes, and reactions.

Then, too, you must be in control of your own emotions, habits, mental processes, and actions as well as your physical condition. You must discipline yourself so that you do not give an opponent a psychological advantage.

Rating You Opponent

Let's discuss, first, your study of an opponent's playing habits in order to take every possible advantage.

Does your adversary revert to "table talk" when playing a card that may start a run? Is he or she baiting you on when he knows that he will gain in the long run?

Does your opponent favor making the opening lead from a pair so that he may score on triplets? Or does he delay the lead until the second series?

Does his play follow any definite routine or pattern?

Does he pair your lead at every opportunity - or does he avoid pairing you with sevens and lower cards only when holding two of a kind, thus setting the trap for quadruplets and 12 holes?

Does your adversary always lead a deuce when he has a trey in his hand, or a four-spotter when holding an ace, to set you up for his 15/2? Your countermove is to play something besides a tenth card when the deuce or four is led, so he can't score with the trey or ace, as the case may be. Furthermore, you have the advantage of knowing one of his unplayed cards.

Does your competitor use playing strategies as used by knowledgeable contestants?

Do you credit him as a very skilful player? If so. you are in a battle of wits.

Has your opponent read this book? If not, you have a great advantage over him.

Conversely, remember that an opponent also observes your habits and patterns of play; so keep out of a rut, and vary your plays. Occcassionaly make an unorthodox play such as opening the series with an ace, to surprise the opposition.

I have heard of a tournament player who keeps records of the style of play utilized by competitors for reference in the next year's tournament.   Such knowledge may be the determining factor in winning a championship.

Conversation

Talk is cheap, but it takes money to buy whiskey!

You must carefully sift the words and remarks that an opponent throws at you during a game as a technique to upset your thinking and play.   Such remarks may be in reverse...complaining with good cards and bragging with poor cards.

False words about the starter card are used by many people. Some players misleadingly delay discarding, trying to convey the impression that they have a problem in selecting a discard.

What should you learn from this discussion? Be poker-faced and keep your mouth shut! Listen and learn!

Worth Two Finesses

There is a saying among bridge and whist players that "one peek is worth two finesses."

In Cribbage too, a peek can give an opponent a slight advantage and cost you the game.

I refer to the opponent who, while cutting the pack for the starter card, sneaks a peek at the card on the bottom of the packet. The rules provide a 2-point penalty for this offense, but pone may steal a glimpse of the bottom card while you are busy deciding on your discard.

So be alert and note if your opponent tips the packet for an unfair advantage.

Memory

Writers have indicated that Cribbage is a different card game in that you don't have to remember the cards played. But this is not entirely true.

It is a good idea to remember the two cards you have discarded to the crib; the information can guide you in the pegging process. Also, remember the styles of play used by your adversaries.

Beware of the Sharpies

Many sharp players will watch the position from which you draw your cards in order to guess the rank of your remaining cards.

Most cardplayers arrange their cards from left to right by suits, with high cards to the left of each suit. In Cribbage, where suits are relatively unimportant, high cards are still placed on the left and lower cards to the right

Q-J-10-2 or 9-8-7-6

If your adversary notes the position from which you draw
the jack in the first example, he knows you have one higher
card, a king or a queen. If you play the seven from the
second example he knows you have two cards higher than
the seven and one card lower.

For self-preservation, watch your opponent's eyes to ascer-
tain whether he is taking advantage of you. And be sure to
mix up the cards in your hand - or simply leave them the way
they are when you pick them up.

Of course, you too can note how your opponent holds his
pasteboards and attempt to read his hand.

Mental Attitudes

Your mental condition has a definite effect on your calibre
of play. Many of us retreat to the card table to forget our
personal problems, at least for a short time.

However, it takes great effort for a person to play normally
when under mental stress.

Here are some don'ts:

1. Don't get frustrated or angry when things are
    breaking badly for you.
2. Don't gamble on uncalled-for long chances.
3. Don't complain about your bad luck or opponent's
    good fortune.
4. Don't argue with opponent.

Positive Thinking

Assume that you are superior to your opponent and be

confident that you are going to win. Then you will compete with a relaxed attitude.

If you are nervous and feel tight, take time out. Take a short walk and get a soft drink or a snack.

Here are some dos:

1. Maintain a happy-go-lucky attitude as it rains one minute and the sun shines the next minute.
2. Forget the games that have been lost and concentrate on the present contest.
3. Stick with the percentages. Over the long pull your skill and the percentages will win for you.

Physical Condition

In major tournaments which require two or three days of intense play, some competitors can be observed spending all their spare time playing cards

They would be better off if they went out for a walk and got some exercise. If tired, you should take a nap and relax. Be sure to get enough sleep at night.

The worst thing to do is to drink alcoholic beverages to excess. Perhaps one drink will help you to relax but cut it off there, as alcohol influences one's judgement, usually causing one to take unnecessary chances. Remember that alcohol may seem at first a stimulant but is really a depressant: you may get tired during the last games of the evening and make foolish mistakes.

WHY THE FIRST DEAL IS WORTH 7 POINTS

Extensive records of games played have been kept since the beginning of the 20th century. Crib addicts have reported results of 500, 1,000, 5,000, and even as many as 20,000 con-

tests. The results tend to vary slightly because of the skill
of the people involved in the studies. As a computer cannot
be used to determine averages accurately because of the
varying decisions players make, the findings of the record-
keepers will have to be accepted.

The combined results indicate that the dealer's hand averages close to 8 holes, the crib 4 1/2, and pegging 3 1/2, for a
total of 16. At the same time, pone should average 10 holes
with a hand of 7 1/2 and pegging 2 1/2.
Pone has the constant problem of trying to balk the dealer's
crib, often forcing the reduction of points held in his own
hand. To be on the average, pone should score 10 points.

In the first round, that is both players having a turn at
dealing, the dealer should have 27 points assuming that the
decimal from the average of 16.2 per hand has been con-
verted into a point. After the second round the dealer
should be on target with 53; the third round 79; and 105 as
the 8th deal is completed. Then too, the turning of a Jack
starter card must also be reckoned with in the overall
averages as dealer usually has five deals per game.

Personally, with having the first deal, I set my sights on 17
holes for the first hand. From then on, 16 dealer points per
hand should hold true.

Pone's strategy on the first deal is to be aggressive and to
score more than 10 points. Pone should know about the 7-
point handicap and should try to reduce the advantage on
the very first deal.

On the other side of the coin, the first dealer, knowing of the
7-point advantage should try to hold pone to less than 10
points.

This discussion is based on average conditions.

The record-keepers have also found out that it usually takes 9 hands to complete a game. Therefore, the starting dealer has 5 deals and 5 cribs, while the opponent has 4 deals and 4 cribs.

The following chart shows why there is a 7-point advantage for the first dealer.

Hand	Each Hand		Running Total	
X	A	B	A	B
1	17	10	17	10
2	10	16	27	26
3	16	10	43	36
4	10	16	53	52
5	16	10	69	62
6	10	16	79	78
7	16	10	95	88
8	10	16	105	104
9	16	10	121	114

Game

Please note that the first dealer will be dealing hands 1, 3, 5, 7, and 9.

Old cribbage players never die, they just fail to count all their points.

BOARD POSITION

The players should have game plans in mind when the game starts. The first dealer's plan is to be dealing for the second time at holes 27, for the third time at hole 53, for the fourth time at hole 79, and for the fifth time at hole 105. And if he/

she is a few holes short after dealing at hole 105, there remains an advantage of the first count on a fifth deal by opponent.

Begin watching the position on the board from the first deal onward. If the first hand is running below average, do your best to keep your opponent from pegging. Try to maintain your 7-point advantage.

Pone, the non-dealer at the start of the game, should realize that his style of play must be aggressive because of the 7-point handicap. It should also be known that pone's average score at the end of the first deal is 10 points. The main objective now is to be dealing at hole 43 for the fourth hand of the game. Average scoring would bring the front peg to hole 36, but that 7-point disadvantage must be made up. One's luck must be pushed by "THINKING BIG".

THE RULE OF 26

The Rule of 26 states that being in Hole 95, the dealer should score 16 points and win with the first count of the next hand. Or let's say it another way--the dealer counts two hands and a crib while the opponent counts only one hand.

In the discussion which stated that the dealer can expect 16 holes on his/her deal and the opponent 10, the dealer should count 26 points to 10 for the adversary. That wins the game if the dealer started at the 95th hole or at a more advanced point. Even though the opponent is at hole 105, the dealer usually wins with the 26 points.

The dealer must do everything possible to score enough points on the previous hand to reach the 95th hole. If necessary, the dealer should pair the opponent's cards even though triplets are expected to be scored. The dealer may have to get into runs to reach that coveted spot. Chances may have to be taken in discarding to hit the big hand. The dealer's attitude should be: It is better to have loved and lost, than not to have loved at all![7]

Translated to cribbage--better to have had a chance to win, than not have chanced at all.

HOW THE EXPERTS DISCARD

In my first book all my secret weapons were not exposed because I anticipated competing in tournament play throughout the country. At one time this writer played in 20 major tournaments a year. Houdini never told anyone the tricks of his trade. Good businessmen do not tell the secrets of their success to competitors. You never get anything for nothing.

As my play in major and super tournaments is becoming less frequent each year, I am sharing my strategies, procedures, and guidelines with the readers of this book. These are plays which the masses are unaware of, despite their years of experience.

Here is my favorite discard for this and similar hands.

$$K--Q--4--3--2--A$$

The average dealer discards the two royal cards into the crib hoping to hit the hand for a 10-pointer. However, the discard of the 2 and 3 consistently nets 7 points in the crib. Keep the royal couple along with the ace and 4 in your hand. There are many discards that the opponent may make that will bring 7 points to the crib. For example, if the opponent tries to balk the crib with a king and an ace and then a tenth card is turned, the hand has a 15/4 and a run of three for 7 points.

A high stakes player from a casino city came to my home for

special instructions. Upon conclusion of the one-day session, he said the 2-3 discard into his own crib was the best stunt that I showed him.

A whole day was spent in revealing secrets of Cribbage to him, stunts he never heard of in 34 years of playing. We played 30 games during the day and this discard came up frequently. He loved it.

MORE EXAMPLES OF DISCARDING

No. 1:   Q-8-7-6-5-A

The 5 doesn't fit with the combinations of 8-7-6 so, as dealer, put the 5 and the queen to work in the crib. In the hand it adds only one point. In the crib with the queen it counts for two points and with a cut of a 5, Q, or any tenth card would be a real point-maker.

An ace always works well with 8-7-6 combinations and frequently brings on a 16--pointer. Then too, an ace starter nets 13 holes for a Raggedy Ann (A-A-6-7-8).

In the pone position, discard the Q-A and go along with the four-card straight.

No. 2:   K-10-9-6-5-4

The mathematicians report that there is a slight advantage of 8 holes for every 48 hands, similar to the above, by keeping the 9 with the 4-5-6. When it does occur in the form of 2 points, it may be the difference of winning or losing a critical game.

No. 3:   9--9-6-3-2-A

When dealing, discard the 6-9 to your crib. When pressed at a bad board position, consider the 3-2 discard.

No. 4:   K-Q-J-10-5-2

As dealer, it is best to discard the two end cards, the K-2. As an opponent frequently lays a king to the crib, there probably will be a couple of points in the crib at least. The hand is more flexible with the king out of it and working in the crib instead.

No. 5:   8-8-7-A-A-A

The discard is obvious. Lay away A-A, regardless of who has the deal.

No. 6   7-5-5-4-A-A

Lay the 5-5 combination to your own crib and the A-A to opponent's crib. Discarding 7-A to the dealer is walking on thin ice.

No. 7:   Q-J-9-7-2-A

Lay the 9-7 to your own crib. It has good chances for improvement because three cards will be added to your layaway.

A-9 discard to the opponent's crib is recommended.

No. 8:   K-K-8-4-4-A

Everyone has experienced more success by keeping the low pair and splitting the high couple. Lay away the K-8.

No. 9:   Q-3-3-2-2-A

Discard the Q-3 because an extra 15/2 is possible with a tenth card being turned, thus scoring 14 holes.

No. 10:

When needing 14 points to win in the pone position you are dealt:

K-J-8-4-3-2

A layaway of K-8 will give you 12 points if a low numbered card is cut.

By laying away the two face cards and holding the 8, a cut of a low card also scores 12 points. However, as 2 holes must be pegged, the 8-3 may provide an opportunity for 31/2.

No. 11:   It is always assumed that the opponent will discard a king to one's crib.

K-Q-J-6-5-4

It is correct to discard the Q-J in case pone gave you a king. Then too, the hand reaches down to a 10-spotter for a run.

Holding a 10 instead of the jack in the above example, lay the Q-10 away. There are chances to hit a scoring hand from the 10 downward.

No. 12:   Have no fear!

Don't hesitate to discard a 5-8 or 5-9 to an opponent's crib to keep your scoring hand.

The combination of K-Q and/or A-2 seldom puts one in great trouble. Once in a while you may get burnt, but don't break a good hand.

A-A is another discard that has to be made at times. Don't fear it and let the chips fall where they may.

SOME TIPS ON THE OPENING LEADS

Students of Cribbage as well as average players often confront the writer with: "You say that a 4 is usually the best opening lead for pone. My grandfather told me that any card lower than a 5 is a good lead. Tell me why you favor the lead of a 4-spotter."

The 4 is a good lead of the low cards because it limits the dealer to three safe plays--9-8- or 7. The lead of a 3 by pone also limits the opponent to three safe cards meaning cards away from runs or from a quick 15/2.

As all rules have exceptions, with a holding of K-4-3-2 lead the 3 with a chance of scoring a 15/2.

Summary of low leads:

Lead of a 4 allows dealer safe plays of 9-8-7

Lead of a 3 allows dealer safe plays of 9-8-7

Lead of a 2 allows dealer safe plays of 9-8-7-6-5

Lead of a A allows dealer safe plays of 9-8-7-6

With regard to the ace lead, however, most players would avoid playing a 7 on an ace lead because of the danger the 7 could be paired for 15/2 and a pair for 4.

It is good common sense for pone not to open play from a pair. Good players pass up the opportunity to pair when the game is proceeding evenly.

Save the lead from a pair for later on as the opponent may be in a no-win situation where pairing is forced. Pone may then score on triplets.

A devious routine by pone may be leading a 3 from K-3-2-2. An enterprising dealer may take the count to 13 in order to score on a pair of deuces after pone makes the 15/2. However, pone upsets the cunning play of "mice and men" by playing a third deuce for triplets.

RESPONSES TO PONE'S OPENING LEAD

1. Pone leads a 2 and dealer is holding K-Q-J-5. Pone probably is holding a 3-spotter. Dealer's play is the 5 to increase the count to 7. That move usually places pone in a quandary as to the next play. His position is now reversed. It is defensive. Dealer hopes pone is forced to play a tenth card which dealer could pair for 2 points. Whatever happens, pone's try for a 15/2 ended in failure.

2. Pone lays down a king for the opening play. Dealer is holding 9-8-7-3. Dealer responds with the 8 and if pone plays a tenth card, dealer plays the 3 for 31/2.

3. When pone leads a tenth card and dealer is holding 8-7-4-A, the dealer should take the count to 17, again having in mind reaching the 31/2 mark. The same strategy may be applied with a 6-5 and a 9-2 combination. The higher numbered card should be played first.

4. Pone leads a 4-spotter. Dealer is holding K-5-4-3. As the lead of a 4 is now being accepted world-wide as an excellent opening play, experts often jump on it with another 4, because in the long run, a person gains by this response. Better yet, if dealer's 4 is backed by a 3, 2 points may be salvaged in case pone scores on triplets.

	Pone	Dealer	
	4		
		4	pair/2
trips/6	4		
		3	15/2

Pairing the initial leads of a 4 is a good percentage play against veteran players.

5. As cribbage devotees are getting more knowledgeable, a lead of a 5 from K-Q-J-5 is being used more frequently. Pone has a 3 to 1 chance that if dealer takes a 15/2 on the response, the royal card played may be paired.

A counter play by dealer with a holding such as J-10-9-9, is to refuse the 15/2 with a 9 making the count 14.

6. In response to pone's first lead of a 9, pair it if holding: (a) 9-4-2-2 or (b) 9-4-4-2

If pone scores triplets with the count reaching 27, there is opportunity of scoring 4 holes on (a) if a person is successful in chancing the 2's. Or holding hand (b), a 4 could be played for a less dangerous but sure 31/2.

7. Pone starts the play by leading a 3. Dealer interprets the lead as a try for a 15/2.

Holding a combination such as J-10-9-6, dealer should respond with the 9, upping the count to 12. The odds favor pone to have a deuce with the 3 rather than another 3. The dealer's odds on the choice are 4 to 3.

8. Pone, in deciding to play a second card responding to the dealer's play, should take a safe pair rather than a 15/2. For instance:

Pone hand: K-Q-4-A

Pone's lead was the 4 and dealer countered with a queen, taking the count to 14. Instead of playing the ace for a 15/2, pone should pair the queen, moving the count up to 24. Thus, there is a chance remaining to score a Go or even another pair with the ace.

THE TRAP PLAYS

The experts have in their bags of tricks a number of stunts to use on their opponents.

THE SIMPLE TRAP

Good players use the simple trap of bringing the count to 29 and hoping the adversary plays an ace for 30. Then play of another ace by the trap instigator nets a 31-count for 4 points.

Similar traps are used with 2's, 3's, and 4's.

The foxes and sharks have a number of more sophisticated traps to entice an average Knight of the Peg to take the bait.

THE FIVE-SPOT TRAP

Mr. Fox traps a five for a run of three and takes a Go for good measure.

Mr. Fox	Mr. Hunter(dealer)
Q-7-7-6	K-Q-5-5
7	
	K
Q(Go)	
	Q
7	
	5
6 (run of 3 and Go)	
	5 (Go)

With his run of 3 and two Go's, Fox out-pegged Hunter 5 to1.

Setting a Mousetrap to Catch a Jack

The mousetrap is a necessary item in many homes and in a
cribbage player's bag of tricks. When a non-suspecting
opponent is caught, the trapper scores 7 points. This stunt
works frequently when an opponent has to discard a tenth
card to dealer's crib. A ten, queen, or king is chosen rather
than a jack which may turn out to score as nobs. People just
don't like to put a jack in dealer's crib.

Mr. Fox, the crafty dealer, holds a pair of jacks and plays off
two low cards to pone's lead hoping that the opponent scores
a Go.

Fox now leads one of the jacks and the opponent, with only
a jack left, scores 2 points on a pair. Fox plays the third jack
for 6 points and takes a Go for a total of 7 holes.

Mr. Hunter	Mr. Fox (dealer)
J-8-8-7 (K-3)	J-J-4-3 (8-7)
7	
	4
8	
	3
8 (Go for one)	
	J
J	
	J for 6 and 1 for Go, 7 holes

It follows then, that pone's defense when holding a jack is to
play it off as soon as the count goes to 12 or more.

THE END-PLAY TRAP

Mr. Fox springs traps from dealer's position.

Hunter	Fox (dealer)
K-Q-J-5	8-7-6-3
Q	
	8
J	
	3 (31/2)
K	
	7
5	
	6 (Go/4)

Fox outscored Hunter 6 to 0 with the end-play traps. Hunter could have avoided the possibility of a trap by leading the 5 on his first play of either series.

THE "MOUSE" TRAP SNAPS AGAIN

Mr. Fox offers Mr. Hunter a piece of cheese in the form of a 3-card run and then scores 10 holes in return.

	Hunter	Fox (dealer)
	9-8-7-6	6-6-5-4
	8	
		6 an invitation
(For 3)	7 (for 3)	
		5 for 4 points
		4 for 5 points

A player must give in order to get!

FOX SPRINGS THE OLD FAITHFUL TRAP

As Mr. Fox entered his favorite bar, he was greeted by a visitor, a Mr. Chase, from Englewood who said: "Mr. Fox, I hear you are the best crib player in town. You may be the best here, but that doesn't cut any ice anywhere else. How about a game?

Fox didn't say anything but got a pack and a board from the bartender and motioned the stranger to come over to the front table. The stranger won the cut and dealt the first hand. As the game progressed, he was leading by a street most of the way.

When Chase entered 4th street, he was the next dealer with only 16 holes to go and Fox had 31 to go. Chase dealt:

Chase	Fox
K-K-K-5 (7-7)	6-6-5-4 (Q-3)

Fox cut the pack and Chase turned a 5 for the starter card.

Fox watched the facial expressions of Chase when the 5 was turned. A big smile had come over the visitor's face. Fox mumbled: "I think I've got Old Faithful!"

This is one hand in which pone's lead of a 4-spotter is a no no. The 6 is the play which Fox promptly made. Here is how the hand went.

Chase	Fox
	6
K	
	6
5	

4 Fox gets a run of 3 and a 31/2 for 5 pts.

With the count at 22, Chase had to play the 5 as he was
trapped.

K

5 15/2 for the Fox--a total of 7 peg pts.

K for a Go

With 24 points left to go and Fox's first count, the 24-point
hand put him in the game hole.

Chase said: "Thanks for the lesson." and took off.

THE DILEMMA OF THE SIXES, SEVENS AND EIGHTS

The valley cards are the 6's, 7's, and 8's. With 13 cards in
a suit, the 7 is the middle card of the suit. It is the fulcrum
which holds the balance.

With a holding of 9-8-7-6 pone often finds himself in deep
trouble if the dealer has a similar combination. It happens
so frequently that pone must be aware of the shortcomings
of the hand as well as the possibilities of increasing the
value from 8 to 16 holes with the cut.

<u>EXAMPLE 1</u>:

9-8-7-6

| pone |
| dealer |

9-8-7-6

The first problem for pone is to decide which card to play
first. Although it is usually better to lead a 6 if holding 6-
9, the above case is an exception.

The usual play is to lead the 8, give up a 15/2 to the dealer, and retaliate with the 9 for a three-card run and 3 holes. Dealer plays the 6 for 4 holes on a run of four and the count of 30 earns 1 hole for the Go.

The net results of that first series is pone 3 and dealer 7 points.

Second series is a repetition of the first series.
To salvage 3 holes, pone leads the 7 and dealer responds with the 8 for 15/2. Pone cashes in on the three-card run for 3 holes, and dealer takes 4 holes for the extended run and 1 for the Go.

The net results of the entire hand is pone 6 and dealer 14 points.

Pone's rationalization is that he didn't have an idea as to the cards held by the dealer, but he did score 6 needed holes.

EXAMPLE 2: A VARIATION

An alternate play to stop the possible runs in such situations, is leading off with a 7 allowing dealer to score a 15/2 with an 8. Pone then pairs the 8 for 2 points, shutting off the possibility of a run.

The Play

9-8-7-6	9-8-7-6	
Pone	Dealer	
7		
	8	(15/2)
(pr/2)8		
	6	(Go/1)

Second Series:

```
        6
                    9        (15/2)
   (pr/2)9
                    7        (Go/1)
```

The pegging for points is radically reduced for the entire hand as pone totals only 4 but keeps dealer down to 6, a spread of only 2 points.

Pone's pairing of the 8 in the first series could be a major disaster if dealer held a third 8, as triplets would yield 6 holes plus 2 more for the Go at 31. In this event, dealer scores a total of 13 holes while pone is on the short end with 4 holes.

This is a percentage play for pone and that is what Cribbage is all about.

EXAMPLE 3: ACE IS AN ASSET TO VALLEY CARDS

An ace is a welcome addition to the valley cards as it helps build high scoring hands and also aid in pegging. Take, for instance, this hand:

8-7-6-A   9-8-7-6

By leading the ace, pone takes the advantage away from the dealer.

Pone		Dealer	
A			
		6	
(15/2)8			
		7	(run/3)
(pr/2)7			
	(Go/1)		
		8	
6			
		9	(Go/1

The net results are entirely different when the ace is a helper. Pone scores 5 and allows the dealer only 4 holes. In the counting of the hands, the starter card may provide help in a number of ways to a hand of three valley cards and an ace. A cut of a 9 scores 10 points; an 8 or 7 nets 16; a 6 makes a 14-point hand; and an ace presents Raggedy Ann, (8-7-6-A-A) and 13 points to the holder.

EXAMPLE 4: KEEPING A DECOY IS A PLOY

A foxy player sitting in the pone position with no immediate position problems often holds a decoy in the place of a 9 or a 6.

With the valley cards, a deuce, trey or a four may be retained to confuse the opposition. The decoy is played as the third card of a series as follows.

Pone	Dealer	
8		
	7	
4		
	?	(What is pone holding?)

EXAMPLE 5: HOW TO KEEP OUT OF TROUBLE

8-8-7-7

Pone must choose a lead from the above hand. The safe play is to lead an 8 because three 8's total 24, and the fourth one is unplayable as it takes the total count over the 31 mark.

The lead of a 7 may result in the opponent scoring 2 for a pair and 12 on four-of-a kind.

EXAMPLE 6: Here is another technique for your bag of tricks.

Clubs: 8-7-6-A   Hearts: 3-2

The brilliant play is to hold the four clubs for a flush with a count of 11 and at the same time having the opportunity of scoring a 20-pointer with the cut of a 7 or 8, and 18 points with a 6 starter card.

EXAMPLE 7: DEALER LAYS AWAY VALLEY CARDS

The dealer, on occasion, may split valley cards and discard them to the crib to retain a better hand.

2-3-4-7-8-9

The right choice in this example is discarding the 7 and 8 to the crib.

A cut of a 2, 3, or 4 increases the hand to a 12-pointer. A cut of a 9 makes it a 9-pointer. On the other hand, the 8-7 in the crib may be helped by three cards, the starter card and the two cards discarded by pone.

EXAMPLE 8: RESPONDING TO A LEAD OF AN 8

Valley cards overlap into other hands as in this illustration of 10-10-9-8. An 8 has been led by pone.

Dealer ruled out the play of a 9 for obvious reasons. And the play of a 10 left an opening for a 9 spot for a run.

The pairing of the 8 was chosen as it is an aggressive move to score 2 points.

EXAMPLE 9: THREE VALLEY CARDS GET INVOLVED
WITH THREE ACES

Pone receives A-A-A-7-8-8 on the deal and chose to give two
aces to the dealer's crib. In an earlier section on discarding,
it was stated not to worry about throwing away two aces.

Pone led a 7 which the experts agree with as a 15/2 can be
scored if dealer pairs it. In the event the dealer makes a 15/
2, pone can pick up 2 points for pairing an 8. Percentage is
definitely in favor of pone in these plays.

EXAMPLE 10: FOUR VALLEY CARDS AND TWO FIVES
CAUSE A DISCARDING PROBLEM

Pone is dealt 7-7-6-6-5-5. What a predicament to be in!

A double run must be kept, but which one? The master
selects the discard of 7-5. It is unlikely that dealer will
throw a six as pone has two of them. A discard of the 7's is
asking for deep trouble and throwing the 5's is suicide.

How about holding the hand in the dealer's position? Discard the two 5's as their future is with the royal cards and
the combination of 7-7-6-6 is open at both ends for some
help.

EXAMPLE 11: A PAIR OF SIXES MAY BE USED DEFEN-
SIVELY

Pone holds: 8-7-6-6

A lead of a 6 is a lesser of the evils of leading from four valley
cards.

	Pone	Dealer	
(a)	8-7-6-6	9-8-7-6	
	6		
		9	15/2
	6		
		6	pr/2 + Go/1
7			
		8	15/2
	pr/2 8		
		7	Go/1

The net reult is that dealer scores 8 points and pone 2 for a difference of 6 holes.

	Pone	Dealer	
(b)	8-7-6-6	9-8-8-7	
	6		
		9	15/2
	6		
		8	Go/1
	7		
		8	15/2
	pr/2 8		
		7	Go/1

The net result is that dealer scores 6 points and pone 2, only a difference of 4.

(c) The Shoe May Be On the Other Foot

Pone		Dealer	
8-7-6-6		6-5-4-4	
6			
		6	pr/2
6	trips/6		
		4	
8	Go/1		
		5	
7			
		5	Go/1

Pone pegs 7 points and dealer 3, pone gains 4 points in this matchup.

WERGIN'S WORDS OF WISDOM

* Trust everyone but cut the cards!

* Study the rules for your own protection

* In order to rise above the masses, board position must guide your play.
  Remember the spots: 17, 43, 69, 95, 105 and out.

* Beware of pairing pone's first lead.

* Do not pair an opponent's card or get into a run down on 4th street if you don't need the points. Thousands of games are lost every year by this stupid mistake.

* The game isn't over until a peg has been placed in the Game Hole.

* Always have confidence in your own play and Think Big!

* And, finally, always keep in mind...when the day comes for you to face the **great scorer and all your records receive their final audit, it behoves you** to have played all your games honestly and fairly with your fellow men and women.

"At   home" means having a normal position on the board in relation to the opponent and to the game hole.

When at home, it is best to play off; when the adversary is safe at home, it is best to play on.

Cribbage is an ideal soothing and relaxing activity for late evening, since it is very helpful in forgetting the trials and tribulations of the day. Try it!

ENCYCLOPEDIA BRITANNICA states that Cribbage is played by over 10 million people in the United States, principally across the northern states from New England to the shores of the Pacific. It is also a favourite game in Canada.

Cribbage is a favourite game in all English-speaking countries.

Another old Cribbage saying is "Here's a piece of cheese" (as a sly lead is made).

The largest room in the world is the room for improvement.

Keep your temper. No one else wants it!

CHAPTER VI

FIVE-CARD CRIBBAGE

ORIGINAL GAME

Cribbage was originally played two-handed in Great Britain, with each player receiving five cards. The old form, which has several notable differences from the six-card game, is considered more scientific but has fewer followers.

In the five-card format, each player discards two cards into the crib and has only three to use in the play.

Game Is 61 Points

A player must score 61 holes to win, instead of the 121 holes for game in the six-card affair. Because of the advantage the first dealer gets from the shorter game, the pone receives 3 points as a handicap or spot, points that are usually recorded immediately after the initial dealer has been determined.

The Go Is Very Important

There is only one Go in each deal. After a player gets a 2-point Go (31 points) or a 1-point Go (last playable card, but under 31 points), the rest of the cards are not played.

Average Scores

The crib can still be expected to yield 5 points, but the average dealer's or pone's hand (with one card less) is worth less than 5 points. In the shorter playing process, dealer can expect to peg 2 points; pone, 1 point plus.

Every point is of great value, because the scoring level is so low. Master players stress playing for the Go, which wins or loses 1 or 2 points.

Balking is Favored

Pone must try even harder to discard two cards that tend to balk or contain the dealer's crib even if it is necessary to sacrifice the scoring potential of the cards retained, because the crib consists of five cards including the starter card, while the hand of each player, again including the starter card, includes only four cards.

In the showing, dealer or pone will very rarely get more than 12 points; but the five-card crib, as in the six-card game, readily scores from 12 to 29 holes.

Watching the Score

Masters of the science of Cribbage are constantly watching the positions on the board with a view toward the objective of 61 points and victory.

A player can expect about 4.5 (hand) + 5 (crib) + 2 (play) = 11.5 points as dealer, and 4.5 (hand) + 1 (play) = 5.5 points as pone. Thus after two deals, the average score is about 17 points for each player (compared to 26 points in the six-card game).

As the game progresses, on the average, first dealer goes ahead by 6 points each time he deals, only to lose this advantage when he is pone. Although this averages out to the 3-point handicap second dealer received at the beginning of the game, in fact dealer has an advantage, as he is likely to reach 61 while dealing before opponent has time to deal and catch up.

By watching the score, player can tell not only if he is ahead but if he's ahead (or behind) as much as can be expected from his current position as dealer or pone. He can adjust his strategy accordingly, either by pushing and speculating or by balking the crib and taking a conservative approach.

Special Regulations

There are a few more regulations that are different in five-card cribbage. Three cards of a suit in dealer's or pone's hand constitutes a flush in the showing: player scores 3 holes, one for each card. If the turned-up card is of the same suit, a fourth point is added. A flush in the crib is counted, as usual, only when all four cards and the turned-up card are of the same suit; such a crib flush counts 5 holes. During the play, flushes are disregarded.

Discarding and Other Tips

You, as pone, should balk, balk, balk the crib. Use the methods discussed at the beginning of part IV under "Basics of Discarding." The crib in five-card Cribbage is the same as in the usual game, so the same principles apply.

Play Cribbage for Fun, for Health, and for Love

If you as dealer have no pair to discard, put down the cards that are as close in rank as possible, hoping that the two cards discarded by pone and the starter card will build a sequence.

Other things being equal, lay out two cards of the same suit for your crib, in order not to eliminate the possibility of a flush.

It is good strategy to avoid breaking up a sequence in dealer's hand; it's especially good when such a sequence is a flush.

Otherwise, tend to favor the crib even at the expense of your hand. Crib hands are larger and higher-scoring. In fact, your only chance of a big catch-up score is in the crib.

WINNING ODDS FOR THE DEALER

One trip around the cribbage board, 61 points, is all that is required for victory in five-card cribbage. Remember, an initial spot of 3 points is awarded to the nondealer at the start of the game.

Odds of the Five-Card Game

Here is an interesting table that was included by Dick and Fitzgerald in their 1886 rulebook of cards, Hoyle's Games. First, situations that favor the dealer are listed; then, even-money situations; and finally, situations that favor the pone.

TIE SCORE (HOLES)	DEALER'S WINNING ODDS
5	6-4
10	12-11
15	7-4
20	6-4
25	11-10
30	9-5
35	7-6
40	10-9
45	12-8
50	5-2
55	21-20
60	2-1

Dealer needs 3, pone needs 4	5-1
15 points of the end	3-1
Same, when 15 of the end	8-1
Dealer needs 6, pone 11	10-1
Dealer is 10 ahead	4.5-1
10 ahead and near the end of game	12-1
Dealer needs 16, pone 11	21-20

ODDS

Player even at 59 holes	even
Nondealer is 3 ahead - not within 20 of the end	even
Dealer needs 14, pone 9	even
Dealer needs 11, pone 7	even

PONE'S
WINNING ODDS

Player even at 56 holes	7-5
Even at 57	7-4
Even at 58	3-2
Dealer needs 20, pone 17	5-4
Dealer is 5 points behind, before turning last corner	6-5
Dealer is 31, pone 36	6-4
Dealer is 36, pone 41	7-4

To fully enjoy Cribbage, the author recommends that you play both the five-card and six-card versions. Our correspondents in England report that in many areas five-card Cribbage remains the favorite.

Oddity in the Five-Card Game

For players who are interested in the unusual and the possibility of freak happenings, here is a situation to analyze.

It is possible for a player who hasn't pegged a single hole and who is 56 points behind his adversary, to win the game 61 to 60 within two deals.

One-Card Discard

An American variant begins like five-card Cribbage in that five cards are dealt to each player - and two cards into the crib.

Each contestant discards only one card to the crib, retaining four cards in his hand. Except for the discard, that variant is played and scored like six-card Cribbage.

Cotton's 1674 chapter on "Cribbage" says that the five-card game played up to 60 points.

Cribbage is a favorite game in all English-speaking countries.

CHAPTER VII

VARIATIONS OF THE STANDARD GAME

Three-Handed Cribbage

When a trio of Cribbage buffs assemble around a perforated wooden slab, there is plenty of action, and the pegs can really fly.

Strategy is complicated by the addition of a third player. In play it is a good idea to favor a trailing adversary at the expense of a leading one.

Early Cribbage freaks constructed a board for threesomes with three separate sets of 61 holes. This evolved into a modern rectangular or oval board with three parallel lanes--a refinement which has contributed greatly to the excitement of the match by displaying the players' relative positions in their struggle to reach the game hole.

Two popular forms of three-handed play are in vogue: (1) each contestant competes on an individual basis, and (2) two join in a partnership against the third person--Captain's Play.

Except as noted, the standard two-handed rules guide the play.

Play as Competing Individuals

1. The first dealer is chosen by the cut of the pack with the low card awarded the deal. In case of a tie the old adage "Two tie, all tie" applies, and all three players cut again until the low person is decided.

2. Number of cards: Each participant is dealt five cards,
one at a time, and a sixteenth card is dealt into the crib. (A
variation is to deal five cards to each player except the
dealer, who receives six cards by taking the sixteenth card
into his hand. Then dealer discards two cards instead of one
as below.)

3. Each player discards one card to the crib.

4. The eldest or senior hand--that is, the player to the
dealer's left--makes the initial lead in the pegging series.
Pone, who sits on the dealer's right, plays the second card,
and the dealer, the third card.

5. The first player reaching the 121st hole is the winner. (A
variation: After a player reaches the win hole, the two remaining participants continue to the finish, thus determining the runner-up.)

6. To keep score, use two regular Cribbage boards; or
better, purchase or construct a board with three lanes of
holes.

7. When a contestant cannot make a play, he says, "Go,"
and the next player to the left must make a play if able to do
so. The turn then moves to the third player until the series
is completed. The Go is scored by the last person to make the
play.

8. The eldest position shows first and records his holes.
Then pone shows, followed by the dealer. Finally, the crib
is counted.

9. The deal passes to the left.

Captain's Cribbage - Two Against One

Captain's play is more interesting and exciting than the individual game for three players. The guidelines of the latter game also guide Captain's with a few exceptions.

Two players compete against one and the lone player must score 61 or more points while the partnership must reach the 121st hole for a win. The skunk line is at 45 for the lone player and at 90 for the pair.

A match consists of three games, with each competitor having a turn at being the lone player. A variation permits the lone player who is skunked to recoup the loss by being the lone player in the next game.

The strategy for both sides is to take every opportunity to pair a played card, and to take advantage of a sequence. Of course, board position should be considered under certain conditions.

An all-star play for the lone player is to lead a 7 when starting the first or second series, encouraging the opposition to take a 15/2 and a three-card run of 7-8-9 or 7-8-6. Of course, the lone player should have a 6 or a 9 to complete a four-card sequence. After enticing the pair on this maneuver, the loner may lead a 7 without a supporting card as a feint or a sham.

When leading with a partner on the left, a 5 is an excellent move to score a 15/2. When leading through the lone player, a low card should be played to setup a possible 15/2.

The world's worst lead for the lone participant is an 8 as a 15/2 by left opponent and a run of three with a 9, nets the pair 5 points or 6 with a Go. Or, they may have the opportunity of making a straight of 8-9-10.

PARTNERSHIP PLAY

Four-Handed Competition

A very competitive but sociable form of Cribbage is played
with partners sitting opposite as in Bridge. During discards
to the crib and during play, partners must be cooperative in
order to garner the most points from their combined cards.

Game is 121 points, twice around the board, and a side is
lurched if it does not get 91 points.

Partners may be decided by a challenge, by mutual agreement or by cutting cards, the two low cards competing
against the two highs.

The Deal

Decide which two adversaries are to record the score, for
only one board used. These two parties cut the pack; the low
card wins the initial deal.

After the cards are properly shuffled, pone, the player on
the dealer's right, must cut the pack. This is important,
because one of the players usually sees the bottom card as
the shuffle is completed. The advantage of knowing one
card that is out of play may decide the contest.

The Crib

The crib is the property of the dealer. Each player pitches
in one card; players and crib then have four cards each.

The left-hand adversary must discard first, and so around
the table, the dealer laying out last. Before you discard,
always know which side owns the crib.

Deciding on just one card to be discarded is seldom difficult. Fives are the best cards to lay out to your own or your partner's crib, but not to an opponent's crib.

In general, low cards from the deuce up help the crib, while kings and aces are balkers or killers. Sevens and eights also help the crib.

If you are confident that the game will be decided during the pegging and that you will not need to show your hand, discarding a helping card to an adversary's crib will not affect the outcome. Split your medium and high pairs and keep the low pegging cards.

The Starter

When the players have discarded to the crib, the pack is cut to select the starter card.

The person to the dealer's left must cut the cards, leaving at least four in each packet. (Note that the right-hand adversary cut the pack before the distribution.)

Dealer lifts up the top card of the lower packet, and the top section is returned to the original position. Dealer then places the card face up on top of the deck.

If a jack becomes the starting card, the dealer's side immediately scores 2 points for his heels.

Scoring

The partnership scores are pooled and recorded on the board by one member of each side. The other two players are not allowed to touch the board or the pegs; however, each may prompt partner and point out any omissions or irregularities found in the computation.

The person who marks scores has a troublesome task. One must maintain constant vigilance in order not to omit scoring points made by partner (marker is less likely to fail to record his own points). Nonmarking partner must acquire the habit of seeing that marking partner pegs the full number gained.

Partners may assist each other in counting their cribs and hands, since their interests are mutual. They should also watch and check all scores that the adversaries claim and record.

To avoid confusion about which cards have been played, turn over all cards in a series after each Go.

In four-handed cribbage, a situation may arise in which neither of the dealer's opponents holds a single point in hand. The dealer and partner, with the assistance of a knave turned up, can make 61 points in one deal, which the adversaries only peg 24 points. Such a situation may occur only once in a hundred years.

Pegging and Strategy for Leadoff Player

The senior hand, in choosing the initial lead of the first series, should exercise great care not only at the start but after every 1- or 2-point Go.

A five is a bad lead because the chances of a tenth card succeeding it are so high; and an ace is seldom a good lead, since a good play for the next player is a tenth card, bringing the count to 11. Your partner cannot pair him without making 21 - a bad count, since the next player can probably hit 31 for 2 points.

The lead of a nine is not recommended because your left-hand adversary may bring the count to 15/2 with a six, and your partner does not dare to pair him since the count would then become 21. It is better to open with a six; if opponent makes a 15/2 with a nine, partner can safely pair the nine, without fear of the opponent scoring triplets (another nine would take the count over 31).

Keep this advice in mind: Never make the number 21 yourself, or compel your partner to do so.

Deuces, treys, and fours are safe leads, which force opponent to set up a possible 15/2 combination for your partner.

The second player must observe caution in pairing a card, in case of triplets. He is safer if he sees one of the two missing cards as the starter card or in his hand, or if he has seen one already played.

Second hand should not play closely on, unless compelled by the cards. If your right-hand adversary leads a three, and you reply with a two or a four, you present your left-hand antagonist with the opportunity of forming a sequence. Playing off with a six or higher card would be safer.

On the other hand, you may play on intentionally, to tempt adversary to form a sequence when you feel your partner can cash in on a longer sequence. Or the board may tell you that a few holes are of paramount value and should be pegged at any risk.

As second player, you are safer hitting 15/2 than pairing the preceding card.

If the score indicates it is crucial to prevent opponents from scoring, second or other player should retain cards that are all wide apart.

Pegging and Strategy for Third Player

The third player should keep the count under 21 so his partner, rather than dealer, has the best chance to get a Go of 31 or under.

Pegging and Strategy for Dealer

As last discarder, don't give an ace, deuce, or trey to the crib.

Playing the Board

Life is based on averages. In sports, key figures can be batting and earned run averages, yards gained per pass received, or percent of free throws hooped; elsewhere in life, the average lifespan, average amount a family spends on food, and so on, are very important. As time passes we see statistics and statistics, and more statistics.

Cribbage players fell into that some obsession many years ago. They studied and compared scores of hands, the pegging, and the crib for four-hundred plays and came up with figures for the average player that are close to those for two-handed play: 7 for the hand, 5 for the crib, and 4.5 for the play. (Experts may average a little more.)

The nondealing partners should each get 11.5 points on a deal. The partnership gets 23 points.

Dealer's partner gets 11.5 points, but dealer gets 16.5 (including 5 for the crib), so the dealing partnership should average 28 points per deal.

Therefore, the following pattern of scoring of progressive totals represents average play, where A and B are first dealer and partner, and Y and Z are first dealer's opponents.

DEAL NO.	A-B HOLES	Y-Z HOLES
1	28	23
2	51	51
3	79	74
4	102	102
5	119	121 and wins

The seating arrangement:

```
┌─────────────────────┐
│        Y            │
│   A          B      │
│        Z            │
└─────────────────────┘
```

A, the first dealer, also deals the fifth hand. On the fifth deal, each side pegs the average 9 points, raising the totals from 102 to 111. The showing of hands decides the game. According to the rules, Y (player to left of dealer) shows first, then B, Z, A, and the crib.

Y shows 7 holes and the Y-Z total advances to 118. B shows 7 holes and the A-B total advances to 118.

Z has 7 holes, so he can move his peg 3 holes into the game hole and win for dealer's opponents.

Predicting the Winner

A slight deviation from average, of course, can allow the first dealer's team to show the crucial crib hand and win.

1. The original nondealers have a very slight edge.

2. They should observe moderate caution in the first hand and pay close attention to the medium hands, which are the bread and butter of the average pattern.

3. They should watch the board continuously and compare their position with the opponents', maintaining an average position.

4. There will be fluctuations - highs and lows that upset averages and make the game more exciting, while suggesting modification of the game plan by using an aggressive offense or a conservative defense.

5. If trailing, team members must take every opportunity for pairing and should try to garner all possible points. With a comfortable lead, they should avoid playing on and should beware of the pairs.

6. On the fifth or sixth deal, if pegging appears to be the deciding factor, a team should retain its best pegging cards, no matter what they have to discard.

LOW BALL OR GIVE AWAY

There are 2 or 3 million Americans playing Cribbage every night, and there is always someone trying to invent a variation.

People get bored with activities or lack of activity when they have a losing streak, so they try to inject some novelty.

Play in Reverse

This variant is just right for the unlucky player who is always on the short end of the score and who believes that his opponents always draw winning cards. The object is to push your opponent to the 121 mark, at which point he loses the game.

As pone, by discarding points to dealer's crib you create favorable pegging situations for him, and you spoil your own hand by retaining as few points as possible. You make all the "wrong" plays on purpose to give opponent the game. And, of course, he loses two games if you can lurch or skunk yourself by not reaching the 91st hole.

A very interesting hybrid!

Auction Cribbage

Auction Cribbage has been played in England and America for five decades.

The crib is up for grabs, and is awarded to the highest bider. Bids in points are made alternatvely by the two adversaries, who are willing to reduce their total on the board for the privilege of purchasing the treasure box.

Included in the purchase price is the right to make the first play of the game, and also the right to show first. Near the end of a game, as scores near 121, possession of the crib as well as the opportunity to count first can be a great advantage, but to get the crib then, you will have to bid high, which serves as an equalizer.

Proponents of this arrangement insist it is the best way to make the game fairer, but we believe the intention really was to add some spice.

Postmortems are the curse of all card games!

An unusual procedure in this game is that the person to the dealer's left cuts the pack to determine the starter card.

Do today's playing today!

When in doubt, lead a four-spotter.

CHAPTER VIII

APPENDIX

THE AMERICAN CRIBBAGE CONGRESS, INC.

This organization was formed at Raleigh, North Carolina on August 6, 1979 and chartered under the laws of the state of North Carolina as a non-profit corporation.

In the application for a charter, the purposes and objectives of the organization were set forth as follows:

1. To foster the spirit of good-fellowship, to increase the interest in Cribbage, and to exercise care and supervision over all affiliated Cribbage organizations and associations in the United States and Canada.

2. To adopt and enforce uniform laws, rules, qualifications, and methods of playing the game, and to govern players, clubs, and tournaments in its membership.

3. To issue sanctions to its membership for club and tournament play, and to collect stated fees as provided by the laws, rules, and regulations of the American Cribbage Congress.

Membership in the Congress provides many benefits to the individual players. Herewith are the important programs.

1. Major tournament are staged throughout the country.
2. Players may earn national Rating Points by excelling in sanctioned tournament play.

3. Holders of 29-point hands in tournament play receive trophies and cash awards.

4. The Congress has established a HALL OF FAME and outstanding Cribbage leaders are elected to receive this great honor.

5. The GRASS ROOTS PROGRAM, which sponsors the formation of clubs in villages and communities, is available to thousands of players.

6. Promotion of Cribbage among the youth is being accepted by educators. A number of school officials invite leading players to teach special classes.

7. The CRIBBAGE WORLD MAGAZINE is mailed monthly to all members. The Magazine lists scheduled tournaments, reports results, features articles on expert play, reports Cribbage-related news, and lists regional and national standings.

8. So that decisions are consistent, tournament judges must pass the rules examination before they are certified.

The Congress is governed by a Board of Directors, who are elected by the membership. Representation is based upon numbers of members in geographical areas. The president and the vice-presidents are elected by the Board of Directors.

Membership increases at the rate of about 500 new members a year. Most members pay annual dues but there is a life membership program for senior citizens.

All officials serve without pay. There is no allowance for travel or other personal expenses.

THE GRASS ROOTS PROGRAM

In the application for a charter to become a non-profit corporation, our founding fathers stated, in part, that the purposes of the new organization were:

A. To generally promote the game of Cribbage

B. To promote and to encourage the promulgation of fair and reasonable rules to govern the game of Cribbage

C. To organize and sponsor Cribbage tournaments

D. To formulate and maintain ethical standards to govern the conduct of its members

In the first few years of the American Cribbage Congress, practically all the efforts were slanted to developing bigger and better state and regional tournaments without much effort to "generally promote the game of cribbage"

Your author, the Founding President, was of the opinion that to promote cribbage generally, it was necessary to reach players in the local neighborhoods and communities by taking tournament play directly to them. This could be accomplished by having the clubs play similar schedules of nine games each week of every two weeks. The results would be sent to headquarters for recording. Winners were to be credited with rating points in a system to be developed.

The President created the Grass Roots Project and assumed the roll of National Commissioner and adopted the commission form of governing, a chain of command. The Commissioner appointed the club director and they in turn, selected their cabinets.

Five leaders representing Madison, Wisconsin; Hermiston,

Oregon; Crystal Lake, Illinois; Santa Maria, California; and
Hamburg, New York, responded to the call and formed
clubs.

The project was an immediate success as the memberships
in the five clubs grew from 12 to as many as 50 players. After
three seasons, there were 26 chartered clubs and record-
keeping required more and more time on the national level.
The President named a new National Commissioner and
under his guidance and new ideas, the total number of
chartered clubs is now on the way to 200.

The system of rating points determines the season's champions, and the top 10% are invited to participate in the
Tournament of Champions which is held annually in one of
the casino cities.

The Grass Roots brings out players with little experience
beyond their family and their small circle of friends. In
Grass Roots, cribbers compete against some players who
have had major tournament experience. Everyone in the
club becomes a better player. The Grass Roots serves as a
farm system to develop players for the major events.

The Commissioner and all the directors of the clubs are
doing a great job in "generally promoting the game of
cribbage: as stated in the original application for the charter.

The author's dream is now to have Grass Roots Clubs in all
the cribbage-playing nations of the world and to have the
card players of other countries adopt cribbage.

HOW TO FORM A CLUB

As nine games are played each session, at least 10 players
should be in attendance. It is recommended that at least 12

players form a local club. Club members are required to become members of the American Cribbage Congress and are to pay a couple of dollars a year toward the administration of the program.

A club should strive to secure at least 20 members to play weekly and a person is free to attend as many sessions as desired. A club must play at least 20 times in a season and not over 40. An advance schedule of the dates must be filed with the Commissioner.

Clubs are accepted anytime during the season. Regarding club size, when a club reaches 60, plans should be made to split into two separate clubs. The ideal number is between 24 and 40.

In the matter of local prizes each evening, the Club decides upon the entry fee and the amount of each award. However, regulations provide that the ratio of prizes be at least 1 to every 5 players, or better yet, 1 to every 4. A suggested schedule of awards is provided by the Commissioner.

The Long Board is the official board and the jumbo size playing cards should be used. An expense fee of $1 each evening will help defray all expenses.

The program is flexible in that clubs can be organized in military installations, on ships, or in foreign countries and compete against the North Americans.

Contact the Commissioner of Grass Roots, American Cribbage Congress, for applications and a copy of the booklet, RULES AND REGULATIONS of the GRASS ROOTS PROGRAM.

HOW TO STAGE A CLUB TOURNAMENT

DRAWING FOR SEATS - Have a blind draw for seating

position. Number slips of paper according to the number of players.

SEATING - Ten or more players at a banquet-style table is ideal with half of them on each side. If there are more players, either add tables or have separate tables of ten or more players.

Number the seats according to the diagram below.

10	9	8	7	6
		Table I		
(1)	2	3	4	5

(captain)

ROTATION - After completing a game, all players move one position to the right with the exception of the Captain or Anchor Position.

No. 1, the Captain, stays in Seat 1 for the entire session. Players rotate around that spot.

In the diagram, player No. 10 moves around the table to Position 2.

NUMBER OF GAMES - For the first few tournaments, play seven games instead of nine. It all depends upon how much time is available. Experienced players should complete a game within 15 minutes.

SCORING - Mark "2" in the Game Won-Lost column for winning the game. Enter "3" if won by skunk or double skunk. Also, record in the Spread Points Column, the number of points by which the game was won. The loser enters a zero in the Game Won-Lost column as well as the losing number of points. Be sure to include Hole Number 121 in the count. Then exchange scorecards and make sure the right figures were entered by your opponent. Sign and insert your Identification Number (ID)--the seat number that was drawn.

At the end of the session, total the number of winning and losing games and enter in the proper place. Then, total the PLUS and MINUS POINTS, enter below and determine the NET spread points.

Official Scorecard

NAME _____

                             SEAT _____

Game No	Game Points	Spread Points Plus	Minus	Opponents Signature	ID No
1					
2					
3					
4					
5					
6					
7					
8					
9					

Game Total   Spread
           + _____
Games   - _____
Won Lost   Net _____

                              Checked By

___ ___ _____
                  Signature

AWARD LIST - In club play one award is made for every four players participating. With 12 players there will be three awards.

> 1st   most Game Points
> 2nd   second most Game Points
> 3rd   third most Game Points

Tie-breakers: First tie-breaker is the actual number of games won. If also tied in that category, the most NET spread points breaks the tie. If the tie continues, break it with the highest number of PLUS points before subtracting the total negative spread points.

CRIBBAGE

OFFICIAL TOURNAMENT

RULES

Code of Ethics

Cribbage is a pastime that provides social opportunities to display true sportmanship and respect for others, without rancor, animosity, or overwhelming self-interest during competition.

In view of the above, the following are considered to be *unacceptable* playing practices and are grounds for suspension or expulsion from the American Cribbage Congress:

- Marking or deforming cards for identification or manipulative purposes.

- Controlling the location of the cards in the pack before cutting for first deal or when dealing.

- Secreting cards for later retrieval, including surreptitiously dropping excess dealt cards from the hand.

- Changing or altering score cards.

- Intentionally playing poorly for the purpose of enhancing the record of an opponent.

- Actions or conversation unbecoming a member of the ACC (drunkeness, abusive language, etc.).

- Initiating a violation of rules for the purpose of gaining an advantage, whether actually gained or not, even though the rules specify a penalty for the violation.

By honouring all American Cribbage Congress rules, a player will have guidelines for good sportsmanship and fair play, resulting in an enjoyable experience for all participants.

Aims and Objectives of the American Cribbage Congress, Inc.

The card game of cribbage was invented about 1635 by Sir John Suckling, a British poet and knight. It has survived, with no major changes, as one of the most popular games in the English-speaking world.

However, as the game developed across the United States, local variations crept in. There was no standardization of playing rules in the tournaments that were beginning to appear all over the nation.

In August, 1979, the American Cribbage Congress, Inc. (ACC) was founded as a non-profit corporation .... to promote the noble game of cribage, to pioneer and develop many programs for the benefit of its members, and to promulgate fraternal friendships among cribbage players everywhere.

Administering to the needs of cribbage players on the North American continent, the ACC conducts a well rounded program that includes:

- Cribbage World magazine, published monthly.
- Tournament Trail (sanctioned tournament list).
- National Rating System for tournament players.
- All-American Awards (Top Ten yearly).
- $100 "29" Award for perfect hands.
- "28" Hand certificates.
- ACC Hall of Fame.
- Cribadier General Honorary Commissions.
- Program for players under 18 years of age.
- Grass Root programs for local Cribbage Clubs.

TABLE OF CONTENTS

RULE I. THE MECHANICS OF CRIBBAGE

Section 1. Object Of The Game
Through selection and play of the cards, to be the first to reach the Game Hole (121 points).

Section 2. Number Of Players
The basic game is for two players and these Rules apply only to two-player game in tournaments sanctioned by the ACC. There are also three- and four-handed versions of the game played with essentially the same rules.

Section 3. The Cards
a. A standard pack of 52 playing cards is used.

b. The four suits are considered equal.

c. The card ranking and pip-values are as follows:

Card	K	Q	J	10	9	8	7	6	5	4	3	2	A
Pip-value	10	10	10	10	9	8	7	6	5	4	3	2	1

Section 4. The Cribbage Board
The cribbage board is used to show the score accumulated by each player during the play of a game (front peg), and the amount of the latest incremental score (difference between front and rear pegs).

Section 5. Outline of Playing Sequence
The following listed sequence is an outline of the actions performed in playing a game of cribbage and is intended for the benefit of those learning the game. It does not include any detailed playing rules, which are specified elsewhere in Rule I and thereafter.

a. Pack is cut to determine which player will deal first in the first game of a match; the low card wins the deal. Thereafter the loser of the previous game deals first.

b. The Dealer shuffles and after a mandatory cut by the Pone (non-dealer), distributes one card alternately to each player, beginning with the Pone, until each has six cards.

c. Each player discards two cards to form the crib, which belongs to the Dealer.

d. The remainder of the pack is cut by the Pone to select a Starter Card, which is used in counting the value of each player's Hand and the Crib.

e. Play Of The Card's

   (1) Players alternately play (place face-up on table) one card at a time, starting with the Pone. A cumulative total of the pip-value of the cards played is announced as each card is played.

   (2) When a player cannot play a card without the cumulative total exceeding 31, that player calls, "Go," and the opponent continues to play all cards possible (not exceeding a 31-count). The player who calls Go plays first in the following 31-count sequence.

   (3) Points are scored during this play of the cards (see scoring chart in Section 7).

f. When both players have played all their cards, the Pone's Hand is counted and pegged by the Pone (see scoring chart). The Dealer then does the same for the Dealer's Hand and then for the Crib.

g. The deal alternates between the players until the game ends, which is when either player pegs into the Game Hole.

Section 6. Definitions

Crib - Four cards (two from each player) set aside for the Dealer to score after the Dealer's hand.

Flush - Four cards of the same suit held in the Hand count four (4) points; five cards of the same suit (including the Starter Card) count five (5) points in the Hand or Crib.

Game Hole - Hole number 121.

Go - Called by a player who cannot play a card without exceeding the cumulative pip-count of 31; the opponent scores one (1) point, or two (2) if reaching exactly 31.

Hand - The cards dealt to each player or the cards remaining after discarding to the Crib.

His Heels (Nibs) - Jack, when it is turned up after the cut as the Starter Card - counts two (2) points for the Dealer.

His Nobs - Jack, in the Hand or Crib, of the same suit as the Starter Card - counts one (1) point.

Judge - A person authorized by the American Cribbage Congress or the Tournament Director who answers questions and settles disagreements of players relating to the rules of play.

Match - One or more games between two players, the outcome of which is a match winner and a match loser. The play of one or more games between two players during tournament qualification play does not constitute a match.

Muggins - The scoring of certain points that one's opponent fails to peg. It has no relationship to penalties. The playing of Muggins is optional with the director of a tournament.

Pair - Two cards of the same rank, such as two Aces.

Peg - A small pin which fits into the holes of a cribbage board; to record a score by advancing the rear peg in front of the front peg.

Pegging - The recording of scored points by advancing the rear peg.

Pone - The opponent of the player who deals.

Score - Any points earned by a player.

Scoring - The earning of points.

Skunk - To win by 31 or more points.

Skunk, Double - To win by 61 or more points.

Starter Card - The card which is cut and placed on the remainder of the pack and which is used in counting the value of each Hand and the Crib.

Stink Hole - Hole number 120; one short of winning.

Straights (or Runs), Single - Sequence of three or more consecutive-rank cards (in any order during play of the cards; e.g., 2, 6, 4, 5, 3).

Straights, Multiple (used only in counting Hands and Crib):

Double-Run - Two three-card or four-card straights, including one pair.

Double-Double Run - Two three-card straights, including two pairs.

Triple Run - Three three-card straights, including three of a kind.

Street - Consists of 30 holes. First Street is the 1st through 30th holes; Second Street is 31st - 60th; Third Street is 61st - 90th; Fourth Street is 91st - 120th.

RULES

145

Section 7. Scoring Chart

Cards	POINTS EARNED	
	Play Of Cards	Hand Or Crib
Jack turned by Dealer as Starter Card	2	-
Jack in Hand or Crib, of same suit as Starter Card	-	1
Combinations:		
Two of a kind (pair)	2	2
Three of a kind	6	6
Four of a kind	12	12
Straights of three or more cards (each card)	1	1
15-count (cumulative pip-count or sum of any cards in Hand or Crib)	2	2
Four-card flush (only in hand)	-	4
Five-card flush	-	5
31-count (cumulative pip-count)	2	-
*Go (without reaching 31-count)	1	-
*Final card played (without reaching 31-count)	1	-

*Only one of these scores can be earned with the play of a single card.

RULE II. MIXING THE CARDS

Section 1. Proper Mixing
The pack must be mixed at least three times with the cards faces down or otherwise hidden from both players. The Dealer is not permitted to look at the bottom card after the last shuffle. If the Dealer should do so, Pone is to remind Dealer of the prohibition and score a two (2) point penalty. The pack shall then be reshuffled.

Section 2. Pone's Right To Riffle and To Shuffle
The Pone has the right to riffle and to shuffle the pack upon request.

Section 3. Dealer's Right To Riffle and To Shuffle
The Dealer has the right to make the last riffle and shuffle.

RULE III. CUTTING THE PACK

Section 1. Number Of Cards To Be Cut
a. When cutting for the first deal of a game, the first player shall remove no less than four cards and not more than half the pack. The second player shall leave at least four cards.

b. When cutting before each deal and for the Starter Card, no less than four cards shall be taken from the top and no less than four left on the bottom.

Section 2. Winner Of Deal
a. The player cutting the lower ranking card makes the first deal of the game.

b. If both players cut a card of equal rank, the entire pack shall be reshuffled and they shall cut again.

c. If a player exposes more than one card, said player shall cut again. If the opponent has already cut, the opponent may keep the card or may cut again at his/her option.

Section 3. Cutting Before Each Deal

a. A cut is required before each deal. Dealer shall place the pack on the table for the Pone to cut. The Pone shall not look at the bottom card of the top packet. Should Pone do so, Dealer is to remind Pone of the prohibition and score a two (2) point penalty. The pack shall then be reshuffled and cut again.

b. After the Pone's cut, the bottom packet shall be placed upon the top packet. It is not permitted to distribute the cards from a portion of the pack. The Dealer shall not look at the bottom card of the pack at any time after the cut. Should Dealer do so, Pone is to remind Dealer of the prohibition and score a two (2) point penalty. The pack shall then be reshuffled and cut again.

c. Should the cut be forgotten, before the Pone's cards are picked up the Pone may remind the Dealer that the cut was not offered and the pack shall then be reshuffled and the cut made. There shall be no re-deal after the Pone's cards are picked up.

RULE IV. DEALING

Section 1. Order Of Dealing

a. The Dealer of the first game of a Match (see definition in Rule I, Section 6) shall be determined by cutting the pack (see Rule III, Sections 1 and 2).

b. If a player deals out-of-turn and the error is discovered before the Starter Card is turned and both players have played a card, the deal is void and the correct player re-deals. If discovered thereafter, the Hands shall be played and the nondealer deals next in that game.

Section 2. Dealing The Cards

a. After the cards are mixed and cut, the dealer distributes from the top of the pack one card at a time, face down, alternately to each player starting with the Pone; six cards are dealt to each.

b. The Pone has a responsibility to observe the dealing and to call attention to any irregularities.

c. The Pone shall not reach for nor touch the cards before the distribution is completed except to use the hand or arm as a backstop to prevent cards from falling off the table while being dealt.

Section 3. Exposed Cards

a. If the Dealer exposes a card or cards while dealing, the cards shall be redealt.

b. If a card is found face up in the pack during the dealing, the cards shall be redealt.

Section 4. Incorrect Number Of Cards In Hand Or Crib

a. Before Both Players Have Discarded To The Crib

(1) If both players were dealt the correct number of cards and one player has discarded the wrong number to the Crib (but the other player has not yet discarded to the Crib), the player who discarded the wrong number shall retrieve those cards and discard the correct number.

(2) If both players were dealt the same number of cards, but less than the correct number, the distribution of cards shall be continued to the correct number.

(3) If either player was dealt the wrong number of cards other than as specified in (2) above, there shall be a re-deal

by the same Dealer. The player with the wrong number must allow the opponent to confirm the count; if the player does not (such as by placing the cards face down on the pack), offender is assessed a backward penalty equal to the lesser of ten (10) points or enough to put both pegs off the board. If the applicable backward penalty is less than ten (10) points, the opponent is awarded points equal to the difference.

b. After Both Players Have Discarded To The Crib

When an error is discovered, a Judge shall be called to interpret this rule and select the appropriate actions specified below. Players should not move any pegs nor any cards after the error is first discovered except under the direction of a Judge.

(1) Before the Starter Card is turned, if it is discovered that the wrong number of cards is held in either Hand or Crib, the action specified in column (A) of the table in subsection c, below, shall be taken.

(2) After the Starter Card is turned, if it is discovered that the wrong number of cards is held in either Hand or Crib, the action specified in column (B) of the table in subsection c, below, shall be taken. The actions specified may include the provision that either Hand or Crib shall not be counted. If these specified Hands or Crib have already been pegged, the points shall be retracted.

c. Table Of Actions To Be Taken

The following table lists all combinations of the incorrect number of cards in both Hands and in the Crib, and the corresponding action to be taken. Columns (A) and (B) list the number of the action to be taken when the error is discovered, respectively, before and after the Starter Card is turned. The actions are defined in the following subsection d.

TABLE OF ACTIONS TO BE TAKEN

| | | | STARTER TURNED | |
| | | | BEFORE | AFTER |
Pone's Hand	Dealer's Hand	Crib	(A)	(B)
Correct	Correct	Correct	Play	Play
Correct	Correct	Too Many	1	2
Correct	Correct	Too Few	3	3
Correct	Too Many	Correct	1	4
Correct	Too Many	Too Many	1	5
Correct	Too Many	Too Few	6	4
Correct	Too Few	Correct	7	8
Correct	Too Few	Too Many	9	9
Correct	Too Few	Too Few	1	8
Too Many	Correct	Correct	1	10
Too Many	Correct	Too Many	1	10
Too Many	Correct	Too Few	6	11
Too Many	Too Many	Correct	1	12
Too Many	Too Many	Too Many	1	13
Too Many	Too Many	Too Few	6	14
Too Many	Too Few	Correct	1	15
Too Many	Too Few	Too Many	1	16
Too Many	Too Few	Too Few	1	17
Too Few	Correct	Correct	7	8
Too Few	Correct	Too Many	18	18
Too Few	Correct	Too Few	1	8
Too Few	Too Many	Correct	1	19
Too Few	Too Many	Too Many	1	10
Too Few	Too Many	Too Few	1	10
Too Few	Too Few	Correct	1	8
Too Few	Too Few	Too Many	1	9
Too Few	Too Few	Too Few	1	8

d. *Actions*

1. The same player re-deals.

2. Play continues. The Crib is dead.

3. Play stops at time of discovery. Without exposing any cards in the Crib, add the needed cards to the Crib from the top of the pack. Play continues.

4. If the Dealer has pegged out prior to discovery of excess card(s), the Dealer is assessed a backward penalty of 15 points from the Game Hole. Thereafter, or if the Dealer has not pegged out, the following actions shall be taken:

- If the play of the cards has not been completed,Pone blindly removes and exposes excess card(s) from Dealer's Hand and play continues.

- When the play of the cards has been completed, the Pone's Hand and the Crib, whether short or not, are counted; Dealer's Hand is dead.

- The Pone selects who will be the next Dealer.

5. If the Dealer has pegged out prior to the discovery of excess card(s), the Dealer is assessed a backward penalty of 15 points from the Game Hole. Thereafter, or if the Dealer has not pegged out, the following actions, shall be taken:

- If the play of the cards has not been completed, Pone blindly removes and exposes excess card(s) from the Dealer's Hand and play continues

- When the play of the cards has been completed, only the Pone's Hand is to be counted; Dealer's Hand and Crib are dead.

- The Pone selects who will be the next Dealer.

6. The excess cards in the Hand(s) are placed in the Crib. If both Hands and the Crib are not correct now, then apply the appropriate rule.

7. Add the necessary cards to the Hand from the top of the pack to make the Hand correct, Play continues.

8. Play continues and the short Hands and/or Crib are counted short in the proper order.

9. Play continues and the short Hands are counted short. The Crib is dead.

10. Play stops at time of discovery. Hands and/or Crib with incorrect number of cards are dead. Correct Hand and/or Crib are counted in proper order.

11. Play stops and any points pegged during play are retracted. The required number of cards is taken from the top of the pack and placed in the short Crib. Correct Hand and Crib are counted; the Pone's Hand is dead.

12. Play stops at time of discovery. Both Hands are dead, and the Dealer counts the Crib.

13. Play stops at time of discovery. All Hands and Crib are dead. Deal passes to next player.

14. Play stops at time of discovery. Both Hands are dead and the Dealer counts the short Crib.

15. Play stops at time of discovery. The Pone's Hand is dead. The Dealer counts the short Hand and the Crib.

16. Play stops at time of discovery. The Pone's Hand is dead. The Dealer counts the short Hand. The Crib is dead.

17. Play stops at time of discovery. The Pone's Hand is dead.

The Dealer counts the short Hand and the short Crib.

18.Play continues. The Dealer chooses any four cards from the Crib.

19.Play stops at time of discovery. Dealer's Hand is dead. Pone's short Hand and the Crib are counted.

Section 5. Imperfect Pack

If a pack is found to have a defect that could affect play, such as missing cards, card with broken corner, obvious visual defect on back surface, or torn card edge, a new pack or card shall be put into play. If discovered after either player has picked up any dealt cards, the deal shall be played to its conclusion before the replacement; otherwise it shall be replaced immediately.

RULE V. THE CRIB

Section 1. Placement

a. The Crib belongs to the Dealer and shall be placed with card faces down on the Dealer's side of the board.

b. Cards placed face down on the table for the Crib and released by the fingers, except for the situation in subsection c, below, may not be retrieved and examined again. The penalty for so doing is two (2) points, and the same cards must be returned to the Crib.

c. Prior to the turn of the Starter Card, if only one player discards to the wrong side of the board, that player is permitted to retrieve the card(s) and re-evaluate the selection.

d. If all four cards are discovered to be on the Pone's side they shall be moved to the Dealer's side, without exposure, unless the Starter Card has been turned and each player has played at least one card. In that event the Crib becomes the property of the player on whose side it lies and the other player becomes the Pone and next Dealer in that game.

Section 2. Exposure
The Crib may not be examined or exposed until the specified time to count it (see Rule IX, Section 2). The penalty for a violation is two (2) points.

RULE VI. THE STARTER CARD

Section 1. Cutting
a. After both players have discarded to the Crib, the Pone shall cut the cards.

b. The Dealer shall turn the top card of the lower packet and place it face up on top of the reassembled pack, as the Starter Card.

c. The Pone shall not look at the bottom card of the upper packet when making the cut. The penalty for doing so is two (2) points and will be taken by the Dealer. The Dealer will also be shown the exposed card.

d. If the cut card (on top of the bottom packet) is found to be face up, it shall be turned over, the entire remaining pack reshuffled, and the cut made again.

Section 2. Exposing More Than One Card
a. If the Dealer exposes more than one card in turning the Starter Card, the correct (top) card becomes the Starter Card.

b. In the above instance, the Pone has the right to see the exposed cards before they are replaced in the pack.

Section 3. Scoring When The Starter Card Is A Jack (His Heels)
a. When a Jack is turned up, the Dealer is entitled to two (2) points.

b. The Dealer may peg out into the Game Hole by turning a Jack Starter Card.

c. If the Dealer plays a card before pegging the two (2) points, the Dealer forfeits them.

RULE VII. THE PLAY

Section 1. The Order Of Play

a. The play of the cards starts immediately after the turn of the Starter Card.

b. The Pone shall play the first card face up on the table, announcing the pip value.

c. Each player in turn shall play a single card and announce the cumulative total of pip values (the count).

d. Each played card shall be positioned so as to overlap that player's previously played cards while keeping the identity of all cards visible. Played cards shall not be turned over before all cards of both players have been played and the Hands counted and pegged.

e. A single card which has been released by the fingers is considered played, whether or not the count has been anounced, and may be retrieved only if it would cause the count to exceed 31.

f. If two or more cards are played together, the card that corresponds to the announced count is deemed to be the card played and the others shall be retrieved. If the count has not yet been announced, or doesn't correspond with any of the cards, the player may select any one of the cards and retrieve the others.

Section 2. Scoring

a. Points are earned during the play of the cards for the

following single or combination of consecutive cards played. The player playing the last card that forms a combination earns the points (see Rule I, Section 7, Scoring Chart).

(1) Pair.
(2) Three of a kind.
(3) Four of a kind.
(4) Straights of three or more cards in any sequence.
(5) A cumulative count of 15.
(6) The last card before player calls Go (i.e. can't play a card that would not make the count exceed 31).
(7) A cumulative count of 31.
(8) The final card played, not making a cumulative count of 31.

b. Points scored during the play of the cards normally must be pegged before the earning player plays another card or calls Go, or a valid Muggins call is made, or the total count of the Pone's Hand is announced. However, when a player's opponent has no more cards or has called a Go, the player may play all playable cards in succession and announce the points scored by each one before pegging the total score at one time.

Section 3. Incorrect Announcements And Plays

a. A player who calls a Go, or who pegs a Go-point on the opponent's call or when the opponent has no more cards, when the player has one or more cards that could be played, may correct that error (renege) up to the time a card is played or a Go is pegged. Thereafter, when the player plays any of the reneged cards, the opponent may claim a renege-error up to the time that player plays the next card or the Pone announces the count of his/her Hand. When the claim is made, a Judge shall be summoned and the opponent may select either of the following options before normal play resumes:

(1) Any cards played after the incorrect calling or pegging of a Go shall be retrieved by both players and any

points pegged retracted. The opponent may then take two (2) penalty points for each card that singly could have been played before the Go was incorrectly called or pegged; the Judge shall confirm how many cards are involved since they need not be exposed.

(2) The opponent may take two (2) penalty points for each card of the player that singly could have been played before the Go was incorrectly called or pegged and those cards become dead (i.e., left exposed and not playable if not already played before the renege was discovered). However, such cards are counted in the Hand.

b. If a player announces an incorrect cumulative count, he may voluntarily correct it prior to the opponent's playing of the next card or calling a Go; thereafter the incorrect count is accepted for the rest of that series and any points pegged as a result are considered earned.

c. If a player's incorrect count announcement is not corrected voluntarily but is challenged by the opponent before the opponent plays the next card or calls a Go, then the count shall be corrected. Also, if the offending player pegged points that would not have been earned with the correct count, that player is considered to have overpegged and the provisions of Rule VIII, Section 4 apply.

RULE VIII. PEGGING

Section 1. Direction
Players shall record their first score by placing a peg in the hole corresponding to their score in:

a. The outside track of holes nearest them on traditional boards (four tracks of 30 holes) or long boards (four tracks of 60 holes).

b. The track nearest them on other types of boards.

Section 2. Zero Hand Or Crib
If a zero-count Hand or Crib is held, the pegs shall not be touched (see Rule VIII, Section 6b).

Section 3. Pegging Incorrectly To The Player's Disadvantage
If the wrong number of points is pegged, to the pegger's disadvantage (ie., underpegging a forward score or overpegging a backward penalty), a correction is not permitted after the player's fingers are removed from the peg.

Section 4. Pegging Incorrectly To The Player's Advantage
a. False Claim Of Game
If a player whose front peg is on Fourth Street scores insufficient points to win the game and pegs into the Game Hole or pegs no points but takes any of the following four actions, the player is considered to have falsely claimed the game:

> (1) Starting to record the game on a score card.
> (2) Removing both pegs, either to place in the starting holes or to retrieve personally-owned pegs.
> (3) Advancing the game-record peg (a peg used on some boards to record the number of games won in a match).
> (4) Standing up and starting to leave, or leaving, the playing position.

b. Penalty For False Claim Of Game
If a player has falsely claimed the game, the following steps are to be taken before play resumes:

> (1) One of the player's pegs shall be placed in the hole corresponding to the points actually scored. If the pegs were removed and the players cannot agree on the position, a Judge shall be called to decide the matter.
> (2) The player is assessed a 15-point backward penalty.

(3) The player's opponent is awarded points equal to the number over-claimed (i.e. to the Game Hole).

c. If the wrong number of points is pegged, to the pegger's advantage (i.e. overpegging a forward score or under-pegging a backward penalty) but less than enough to claim the game, before the opponent has played the next card or indicated the acceptance of a pegged Hand or Crib:

(1) Upon discovery by the opponent, the peg shall be moved back to the correct hole and the opponent scores the amount of the error.

(2) If the offender discovers the error, that player may move the peg back to the correct hole without penalty, but shall tell the opponent before doing so.

d. During the play of the cards, if an incorrect pegging claim is not made before the claimant plays another card, or in the event the claimant has no more cards, before the Pone pegs the total count of Pone's Hand, it stands as pegged.

e. During the counting of Hands and Crib, after a pegged score has been accepted (see Rule IX, Section 2) a claim of incorrect pegging cannot be made on that score.

Section 5. Improperly Removing Pegs

a. If a player removes only his/her front peg when there is a score that has not been pegged, then:

(1) If the player completes recording the score in the wrong direction and releases the peg, both pegs shall remain where they are and that score and the previous score are forfeited. If the traditional (four tracks of 30 holes) or long board (four tracks of 60 holes) is being used, and a player pegs from First Street back to Fourth Street, upon discovery the peg on Fourth Street is placed behind the peg on First Street. In the event both pegs end up on Fourth Street, upon discovery they shall be removed

from the board and the player shall start from the zero
hole again.

(2) If the mistake is recognized before the peg is released,
then the peg-in-hand becomes the rear peg and only the
latest score may be recorded (i.e., there is forfeiture of
only the previously recorded score).

b. If a player whose front peg is not on Fourth Street
removes both of his/her pegs when there is a score to record,
then the front peg shall be replaced where it was. If the
players cannot agree where it was, a Judge shall be summoned to decide the matter. After the front peg is replaced
the other peg shall be placed behind it; the unpegged score
is thereby forfeited.

Section 6. Improperly Touching Pegs
A two (2) point penalty is assessed against a player who:
a. Touches an opponent's peg.

b. Touches the player's own peg when there is no score to
peg, except after receiving the opponent's approval to
tighten a loose peg or has notified the opponent that the
player intends to correct an overpegged score.

Section 7. Dislodging Pegs
If a player accidentally dislodges his/her front peg, it shall
be placed back in the hole where it belongs. If there is
uncertainty as to the proper hole, the peg shall be placed as
agreed upon by both players. If the players do not agree, a
Judge shall be summoned to decide the matter. Or, if two or
more pegs are dislodged and the players disagree where the
pegs belong, summon a Judge.

Section 8. Pegging With Opponent's Pegs
a. If a player records points by advancing the opponent's
peg or pegs, they lose those points and the opponent keeps
them. There is no additional penalty for touching the
opponent's pegs.

b. If the player notices the error before releasing the opponent's peg, he/she may return that peg to the proper place and then record the points with their own peg. In this case however, the opponent is awarded two (2) penalty points (see Rule VIII, Section 6a).

c. If the player records points by mistakenly moving the opponent's peg in the wrong direction, the peg shall be returned to its proper hole and the non-offender shall score two (2) penalty points (see Rule VIII, Section 6a). The offending player forfeits the points of the play, Hand, or Crib in question.

Section 9. Recording Score In Opponent's Track
If a player records his/her score but inadvertently places the peg in opponent's track it shall be moved to the proper track without penalty.

Section 10. Failure To Peg Out
a. If a player scores sufficient points to claim the game but fails to peg any of those points, any of the following actions by the player shall cause forfeiture of that score:
   (1) Mixing any of the scoring cards with other cards.
   (2) Starting to record the game outcome on a score card.
   (3) Removing both pegs, either to place in the starting holes or to retreive personally-owned pegs.
   (4) Advancing the game-record peg (a peg used with some boards to record the number of games won in a match).
   (5) Standing up and starting to leave, or leaving, the playing position.

b. Upon the occurrence of any one of the five actions listed in subsection a above, the player's opponent shall immediately notify the player of the failure to peg out. A Judge shall be called and the following actions shall be taken, as applicable:

(1) If the player's pegs have been moved from their previous position, the front peg shall be replaced where it was. If the players cannot agree where it was, a Judge shall be summoned to decide the matter. After the front peg is replaced, the other shall be placed behind it.

(2) If the Starter Card has been mixed with other cards it shall be retrieved if remembered; if not, the Judge shall cut another one.

(3) If the cards were being played when the failure to peg out occurred, then after actions (1) and/or (2) have been completed if applicable, the play shall continue. If the player at fault has mixed his/her unplayed cards with other cards, the opponent shall play his/her cards alone.

(4) After actions (1), (2) and (3) have ben completed if applicable, any previously unpegged Hand or Crib scores shall be pegged in the normal sequence. If cards of either Hand or Crib have been mixed with other cards, the provisions of Rule IX, Section 4 shall apply.

RULE IX. COUNTING AND RECORDING HAND AND CRIB SCORES

Section 1. Exposure While Counting
While counting a Hand or Crib, the cards shall remain on the table, plainly visible to the opponent.

Section 2. Order of Counting
The counting and pegging of the Hands and Crib shall be done in the following sequence. Each step must be completed before the next is started.

a. The Pone shall count his/her Hand first, announcing the total, and peg the score. Pone shall leave cards face up until the Dealer indicates acceptance of the Pone's pegging either verbally or by beginning to count his/her Hand, or any claim of over-pegging is resolved.

b. Next the Dealer counts his/her Hand, announces the total, and pegs the score. Dealer shall then place Dealer's Hand on the Pone's side of the board, still face up. If the Pone accepts the Dealer's pegging, Pone indicates that either by accepting verbally or by mixing the Hand with other cards.

c. Finally the Dealer exposes the Crib, counts it, announces the total, and pegs it. Dealer shall then place the Crib on the Pone's side of the board, still face up. If the Pone accepts the Dealer's pegging, Pone indicates that either verbally or by mixing the Crib with other cards.

Section 3. The Starter Card

a. While counting a Hand, the Starter Card must remain segregated from the Hand. If either player intermingles the Starter Card with his/her Hand, the pack, or Crib, that player is penalized two (2) points and it shall be segregated again.

b. While the dealer counts his/her Hand and Crib, the Pone may remove the pack, leaving the Starter Card where the pack was, and begin the shuffle for the next deal. Should the Pone mix the Starter Card with the pack, Pone is penalized two (2) points and shall retrieve the card. If there is disagreement on the card, summon a Judge.

Section 4. Mixing Hand With Other Cards

a. If a player mixes his/her Hand with the Crib or pack before it is counted and pegged, and before the opponent has confirmed the count (see Rule IX, Section 2), the player forfeits the count of the Hand.

b. If the Crib is involved and the Dealer commits the offense, the Dealer forfeits the Crib count also.

c. If the Pone commits the offense, the Pone is penalized two (2) points and the Dealer is permitted to retrieve the Crib and peg its value. If there is disagreement on the cards, summon a Judge:

(1) The Judge shall assist in the reconstruction of the Hands by recounting and scoring them in an attempt to determine which cards were placed in the Crib.

(2) The cards which the players recall shall be retrieved. If a full Crib is not recollected and retrieved, the Judge shall shuffle the remaining stock and cut out the number of cards required to constitute a full Crib.

Section 5. Assistance In Counting
No aid from a pony, or scoring chart, or any person is permitted in counting Hands, Cribs, or any scores during the play of the cards.

RULE X. MUGGINS

Section 1. When In Effect
a. Muggins is the only optional rule (see definition in Rule 1).
b. Officials in charge of tournaments, leagues, or other forms of organized play shall announce, prior to beginning play, whether or not Muggins is in effect.

Section 2. Situations Which Do Not Apply
a. The omission or underpegging of a penalty.
b. The omission or underpegging of a Muggins score.
c. The dealer's failure to peg two (2) points for turning a Jack as a Starter Card.
d. Points lost by a player by pegging backwards or removing a front peg.
e. A score forfeited for the failure to peg out or for removing both pegs (see Rule VIII, Section 5b and Section 10).

Section 3. Situations Which Apply

Underpegging of all points, to their full value, during the play of the cards and in the Hand or Crib, regardless of the number of points required to reach the Game Hole.

Section 4. Calling Muggins

a. The caller shall state: "Muggins for (number) points". During the play of the cards, the score not pegged or under-pegged shall be identified. If the opponent does not agree, a Judge shall be called. If the true amount of underpegging is determined to be other than the amount originally claimed, the caller is entitled only to the lesser of the claimed and true amounts. The Muggins points shall be scored after agreement or a Judge renders a decision.

b. For points missed during the play of cards, a Muggins call must be made:

 (1) After the player finishes underpegging the score, or if no score is pegged, after the player forfeits the score (see Rule VII, Section 2).

 (2) Before the scoring player pegs a subsequent score or the Pone's Hand is pegged.

c. For points missed in a Hand or Crib:

 (1) The Dealer must call Muggins after the Pone has finished pegging the score or stated there is no score, and before the Pone's Hand is mixed with other cards or the total count of the Dealer's Hand is announced.

 (2) The Pone must call Muggins after the Dealer has completed pegging the Hand (or Crib) score or stated there is no score, and before the Pone mixes the Hand (or Crib) with other cards.

d. The Zero-Count Hand Or Crib

Once a player claims no count in a Hand or Crib, Muggins may be called immediately. After the player's opponent says the word, "Muggins," the player may not correct his count.

RULE XI. PENALTIES

Section 1. Scoring Penalties
a. Penalty points are scored by the opponent of the offending player unless they are specified to be backward penalties, in which case the offender pegs backward the amount of the penalty.

b. The retractions of scores already pegged and corrections of scores overpegged (see Rule VII, Section 3a (1), and Rule VIII, Section 4) are not considered as penalties but as corrections. As such, the rules relating to incorrect pegging are not applicable and any initial pegging errors of such corrections are to be simply corrected.

c. Penalty points should not be confused with Muggins.

Section 2. Mispegging A Penalty
The incorrect pegging of penalties is subject to the same rules as apply to other scores (see Rule VIII, Sections 3 and 4).

Section 3. No Penalty On A Penalty
Under no condition shall a penalty be inflicted due to an error in calling or pegging a penalty.

Section 4. Refusal To Conform To The Rules
Any player who wilfully refuses to conform to any rule after being informed of it by a Judge is not permitted to continue playing in the event; any game or match in progress is forfeited and the winner is awarded a win by ten (10) spread points.

RULE XII. SITUATIONS NOT COVERED IN THESE RULES

In the event of a dispute which is not provided by these rules, the Judges of the event shall be summoned and their decisions shall be final for that tournament.

RULE XIII. AMENDMENTS

Recommendations for amendments to these rules shall be submitted in writing to the Rules Committee which will discuss, prepare and present all rules amendments to the Board of Directors for final approval.

SANCTIONED TOURNAMENT PLAYOFFS

The American Cribbage Congress specifies that in a sanctioned tournament, the top 25% shall playoff for the championship of that tournament (unless a different format has been approved by a Tournament Commissioner). Following are proper playoff pairings for tournaments, according to their size:

Up to 32 players
1
8
5
4
3
6
7
2

Up to 128 players	
1	3
32	30
16	14
17	19
9	11
24	22
25	27
8	6
5	7
28	26
12	10
21	23
13	15
20	18
29	31
4	2

Up to 256 players			
1	5	3	7
64	60	62	58
16	12	14	10
49	53	51	55
24	13	22	19
41	52	43	46
28	25	26	27
37	40	39	38
32	29	30	31
33	36	35	34
20	21	18	23
45	44	47	42
9	17	11	15
56	48	54	50
8	4	6	2
57	61	59	63

Up to 64 players	
1	3
16	14
9	11
8	6
12	7
5	10
13	15
4	2

For larger tournaments: Simply double the 256-bracket, alternating the qualifiers in a descending order between upper and lower brackets.

Byes: If the tournament does not have a full bracket (i.e., 100 players=25 qualifiers), then the top 7 players would draw a bye in a 128-player bracket. Another example: 220 players =55 qualifiers. The top 9 players would receive a bye in a 256-player bracket.

BIBLIOGRAPHY

1674   *The Complete Gamester*, by Charles Cotton

(?)   *Card Games Up-to-Date*, by Charles Roberts (London

(?)   *Hoyle's Games*, by Charles Jones (London)

1882   *Cribbage*, by William H. Green (reprinted by Gamblers Book Club of Las Vegas, Nev.,1975)

1886   *Hoyle's Games*, by Dick and Fitzgerald

1901   *Cribbage*, by Berkeley (London)

1903   *The Standard Hoyle* (Excelsior Publishing)

1910   *American Encyclopedia* (Frank K. Perkins)

(?)   *Popular Card Games* (London: Foulsham & Co.)

1925   *The Complete Gamester*, by Cavendish

1937   *Games for Two*, by Gloria Goddard and Clement Wood

1943   *Official Rules of Card Games* (U.S. Playing Card Co.)

1945   *The Complete Card Player*, by Albert Ostrow

1948　　*Cribbage as I Think It Should Be Played*, by
　　　　Allen J. Jarvis (Branden Press)

1956　　*The New Complete Hoyle*, by Albert H. More
　　　　head, Richard L. Frey, and Geoffrey Mott-Smith

1961　　*Encyclopedia Britannica*, P.687; "Cribbage, a
　　　　Game of Cards" according to John Aubrey.

1971　　*All About Cribbage*, by Douglas Anderson

1974　　*Cribbage Is the Name of the Game*, by Richard
　　　　E. Lowder

1975　　*The Skilful Play of Cribbage*, by Heines House

1977　　*Games & Puzzles* magazine, "Jack in the Box"
　　　　(May) and "Cribbological Postscripts" (July),
　　　　articles by David Parlett

1977　　*Encyclopedia of Games*, by John Scarne

1977　　*The New Cribbage Games*, by Leo A. Blom

1980　　*How to Win at Cribbage*, by Joseph Petrus
　　　　Wergin

1990　　*Cribbage for Kids*, by Joseph Petrus Wergin

Books by Joseph Petrus Wergin

How to Play Skat	1942
Wergin on Skat and Sheepshead	1975
How to Win at Cribbage	1980
Euchre According to Wergin	1990
Cribbage for Kids and Everyone Else	1990